EMPOWERED!

Reclaiming the Meaning
of Missions
Through the Power
of the Holy Spirit

Esther Burroughs

EMPOWERED!

Reclaiming the Meaning of Missions Through the Power of the Holy Spirit

Esther Burroughs

Woman's Missionary Union, SBC
Birmingham, Alabama

About the writer

Esther Burroughs works at the Home Mission Board as a consultant with women, and lives in West Palm Beach, Florida, with her husband, Bob. She travels frequently, is in demand as a speaker, and has the distinct ability of communicating to all age groups. Esther's honesty and insight touches hearts and changes lives. She's the mother of two grown children and the grandmother of her namesake, little Anna Esther. She enjoys needlework, writing, and walking.

Published by:
Woman's Missionary Union, SBC
P.O. Box 830010
Birmingham, Alabama 35283-0010

Scripture verses taken from:
Good News Bible—Old Testament: Copyright © American Bible Society 1976; New Testament: Copyright © American Bible Society 1966, 1971, 1976. Used by permission. Holy Bible, New International Version. Copyright © 1973, 1978, 1984 International Bible Society. Used by permission of Zondervan Bible Publishers.
King James Version
Excerpts from New American Standard: Copyright © 1960, 1962,1963, 1968, 1971, 1972, 1973, 1975, 1977 by The Lockman Foundation. A Corporation not for Profit, La Habra, CA. All rights reserved, printed in the United States of America. Used by permission.

Dewey Decimal Classification: 266
Subject Headings: Missions
                  Holy Spirit

ISBN: 0-936625-90-2
W903106 • 5M • 0191

Contents

Responding to the Holy Spirit 9

Relying on the Holy Spirit as the Source of Power 23

Reclaiming the Meaning of Missions 35

Recognizing and Providing Entry Points for
Personal Involvement 49

Realizing the Diversity of the World and
Risking Involvement 63

Renewing in the Spirit Through Prayer 81

Teaching Plan for Group Study 89

Preface

What do you think of when you hear the word *missions?* foreign missionaries in bush jackets and pith helmets? home missionaries in inner-city New York or Los Angeles? How about the woman next door who doesn't know Jesus? or the teen at the checkout counter in the grocery store?

Simply put, missions is sharing God's love and plan of salvation with persons who do not know Him. Through the Holy Spirit we are empowered to risk and make a difference in the world. Why, then, must we reclaim the meaning of missions? Have we lost sight of what missions is?

Perhaps so. Do you consider missions your responsibility? Or do you relegate it to the home and foreign missionaries we send out?

Jesus said, "Go ye therefore, and teach all nations, baptizing them in the name of the Father, and of the Son, and of the Holy Ghost: Teaching them to observe all things whatsoever I have commanded you: and lo, I am with you alway, even unto the end of the world" (Matt. 28:19-20 KJV). His command to *go* is for everyone. Have you taken it seriously?

Empowered! asks us to respond to the Holy Spirit by relying on His power. It is an account of persons who have taken the command to go seriously and are risking to impact the world with the gospel. Their stories will challenge you to rethink your commitment to our Lord and help you to recognize ways you can enter into a more personal missions involvement. Plus, you'll discover the impact of the great empowering element called prayer. Responding, relying, reclaiming, risking—missions does demand something, doesn't it? Are you ready?

1
Responding to the Holy Spirit

I just saw a golden leaf, carried by the wind, tossed around, and laid quietly on the ground. There have been other times when I've heard the wind blowing through the trees, almost speaking as it blew. And then, on other occasions, the wind has been so strong, I have been afraid.

The Word of God says the Holy Spirit is like the wind. John 3:8 says, "The wind blows wherever it pleases. You hear its sound, but you cannot tell where it comes from or where it is going. So it is with everyone born of the Spirit" (NIV). From this verse we learn that the Spirit has freedom and mystery. The Spirit, in the Greek, is *PNEUMA*, and it moves about just as freely as the wind. We will never see the end of it, nor fully know or understand it.

The Spirit is at liberty to move about exactly as He pleases. The Spirit works to regenerate and to draw people to God. The movement of the Holy Spirit is mysterious, like the wind. We cannot see the wind, but we can see the results of the movement of the wind, such as bending limbs or a free-falling leaf. Likewise, we cannot see the Spirit. We can only see the results of the Spirit's work, such as the changed life of a person who has been born again. But the freedom and mystery of the Spirit suggests that He is divine, because only God is utterly free and utterly mysterious.

I hope you will discover in the pages of this book that God's Spirit within us moves freely through us. Our Scripture theme for this book is found in Ephesians 3:20, which just happens to be one of my "life verses." I cannot tell you the number of times that God has used this verse in my journey. Let's look at the larger passage where verse 20 is found. "For this reason, I bow my knees before the Father, from whom every family in heaven and on earth derives its name, that He would grant you, according to the riches of His glory, to be strengthened with power through His Spirit in the inner man" (Eph. 3:14-16 NAS). That's the Holy Spirit—in the inner man, in you and me. "So that Christ may dwell in your hearts through faith; and that you, being rooted and grounded in love, may be able to comprehend with all the saints what is the breadth and length and height and depth, and to know the love of Christ which surpasses knowledge, that you may be filled up to all the fullness of God. Now to Him who is able to do exceeding abundantly beyond all that we ask or think, according to the power that works within us, to Him be the glory in the Church and in Christ Jesus to all generations forever and ever. Amen" (Eph. 3:17-21 NAS).

Everything that the Holy Spirit does points to Jesus Christ and His work. I love the above passage, because it says that He gets the glory **in the church** in Christ Jesus. This is an important truth for us to understand as we look at our responses to Him.

"Clothe Me with Your Spirit"

Some time ago, I was captivated by the thought in Judges 6:34 of the Spirit of God coming upon Gideon. The Spirit of the Lord "came upon Gideon," which literally means "clothed

Gideon." Remember that the angel of the Lord appeared to Gideon on the threshing floor, and Gideon was absolutely terrified and awe-struck because he had great respect for the holiness of God. Literally, the text says, "The Spirit of Yahweh 'dressed Himself' with Gideon." The human agent became the outer appearance through which the Spirit worked. As I read this, the truth grabbed my heart. I prayed, "O God, clothe me with Your Spirit!" I then envisioned God's Spirit clothing me. Now, each new day I breathe this prayer: "Oh God, clothe me today with Your Spirit." Then, I envision God's Spirit clothing me. Think about that! It is awesome! I am clothed with God. I like the idea of God clothing me and wrapping Himself around me, and indeed, He does just that!

The other side of this truth is that God clothed Himself with Gideon and set about doing His work through Gideon! God dressed Himself with Gideon that day in order to get His work done. Just imagine what He could do with you and me if we understood what the Holy Spirit wants to do through us. The Spirit of God disguised Himself in Gideon. And what a surprise that was for the Midianite Army!

So God and I, in our walk in this world, are clothed in and with each other, living daily in each other. In other words, I walk into my world clothed (dressed) with the Spirit of God, and God walks into my world clothed (dressed) with me. Isn't that incredible! Consider what God can do in your life through the power of the Holy Spirit because He has clothed Himself with you. Child of God, this is what it means to be *empowered* by His spirit.

This same idea is found in Romans 13:14. "Rather, clothe yourselves with the Lord Jesus Christ, and do not think about how to gratify the desires of the sinful nature" (NIV). Paul is saying to Christians that we need to put on a Spiritual nature. Putting on the Spiritual nature is described as putting on a new garment—Jesus Himself. When clothed with Him, people should seek to live according to His guidance, rather than by following the old nature of the flesh. Paul reminds us in Ephesians 6:10-18 that we are to put on the full armor of God. We are to clothe ourselves with the breastplate of righteousness, the shield of faith, the helmet of salvation and the Sword of the Spirit, which is the Word of God. The Old Testament reference to being clothed by God fits beautifully with the New Testament reference. Paul uses a metaphor of a soldier for our comparison and gives only one offensive weapon: the Word of God, as God's Spirit gives to God's people.

"Ain't You Got Power?"

My friend and mentor, Pitts Hughes, tells about the time she was chaplain to student nurses at a hospital in Birmingham, Alabama. Tired and disgusted after a long day's work, she threw her things on the bed and said, "For all the good I'm doing here, I might as well go home." A conversation followed between Pitts and Dowella, a small, frail cleaning woman who worked in the dorm.

Dowella asked Pitts, "Who's inside of you?"

"God," said Pitts, "a God of love, self-control, and power."

Dowella looked straight into Pitts' eyes and said, "If God's Spirit is inside of you, and He's all power, ain't you got power?"

You see, the Spirit that lives inside of us is the secret. Dowella's idea may not have been stated the best way grammatically, but it is profound theology. Dowella understood Who the Holy Spirit is and what Jesus promised us through this Holy Spirit when He left us. In John 14:16-17, Jesus said, "And I pray the Father, and he shall give you another Comforter, that he may abide with you for ever; even the Spirit of truth; whom the world cannot receive, because it seeth him not, neither knoweth him: but ye know him; for he dwelleth with you, and shall be in you" (KJV).

My phone rang one day, and immediately, I recognized their voices. It was Ruth and Ida, two delightful friends and saints of God who are my prayer partners. Each month I give them my travel schedule, and they pray for my engagements and my travels every day. Of course, following each trip, I call them to let them know what God did through us! Our sharing began a journey that was new to me. That day as we shared on the phone about a concern in my life, Ruth began to talk with the Heavenly Father about the matter. Then in a moment, she resumed our conversation. I was pleasantly refreshed. Of course God can be heard over long-distance connections. Being so comfortable with the Source of the power in our lives, we can be in constant conversation with the One Who empowers.

What happened on the phone that day should not have surprised me. God, the God of Abraham, Moses, and Joshua, lived in His people. This God keeps saying, "I will never desert you, nor will I ever forsake you" (Heb. 13:5 NAS). This promise from Hebrews is a triple negative: **Never** will I leave you; **never** will I forsake you, no, not **ever**. Right now, get your Bible, and find John 14:15-17. Write your name in the verse every time you see the word *you*. Pray now, asking the Spirit to clothe Himself with you. Remember that the Spirit of God came upon Isaiah in the year that King Uzziah died, and He came upon Jeremiah at the potter's house. As the Spirit of God came upon these men, they were obedient to what the Spirit of God asked them to do. I want us to realize that as the Spirit of God has come upon us, He has asked us to be obedient and to bear witness of Him in the world in which we live.

"Child-like Wonder"

Have you ever been surprised by the Spirit of God? He rarely comes when we expect Him. Most often, He comes when we least expect Him and often in very illogical ways. As a Christian, how exciting it is to be ready whenever the Lord chooses to surprise us. This certainly gives us an attitude of "child-like wonder," which I think the Spirit of God wishes for us to have: an absolute awe of Who He is and what He might do through our lives.

The God of the Old Testament led His people by walking before them. Remember when David wanted to build a temple for God? It was a worthy idea, but God's response was blunt. "You're not the one to build a temple for me!" He said. He reminded David that from the time He rescued the people of Israel from Egypt until then, He had never lived in a temple; He traveled around in a tent or a "living tent" (2 Sam. 7:5-7). God did not need a place or temple to meet His people, for God Himself dwells in the temple He made. First Corinthians 3:16 says, "Don't you know that you yourselves are God's temple and that God's Spirit lives in you?" (NIV). If anyone destroys God's temple, God will destroy him, for God's temple is sacred, and YOU are that temple! For us to understand that the Holy Spirit empowers us and lives in us is an awesome truth upon which to act.

Signs and Wonders

Often the Bible pictures God as a loving Father. We understand the Son because if we know Jesus Christ as our personal Saviour, we know what God's Son did on our behalf on the cross. If we understand God the Father and God the Son, then we know that the purpose of God, the Son, is to redeem us, allowing God, the Father, to adopt us as children in Christ Jesus. But then we give lip service to the fact that God is also the Spirit. We believe and act in faith with God, the Father, and God, the Son, but **rarely** do we act in faith with God, the Holy Spirit. We seem to be uncomfortable with the Spirit part. We are not quite certain what the Spirit does.

We cannot talk about the Holy Spirit without looking at what happened in the book of Acts. This book tells us that God started something in Jesus Christ that could not be stopped. Luke teaches us in Acts about the Holy Spirit: He provides power (Acts 1:8), boldness (Acts 5:29), and character (Acts 6:3). "Signs and wonders" is a phrase used over and over in Acts. God's Spirit empowered the disciples to do these signs and wonders in the name of the Father.

In Acts 1:7-8, Jesus is standing and talking with the disciples, and they ask Him if He is going to set up His Kingdom

14

or restore the kingdom of Israel: "He said to them: It is not for you to know the times or dates the Father has set by his own authority. But you will receive power when the Holy Spirit comes on you; and you will be my witnesses in Jerusalem, and in all Judea and Samaria, and to the ends of the earth" (NIV). When Jesus met with His disciples for that final time, He provided a "walkway" or bridge between His earthly ministry and what He would do through His Spirit indwelling and empowering His disciples. He promised His power to do exactly what He desired His disciples to do.

Acts 1:8 tells us that the Holy Spirit came upon the disciples, fulfilling the promise that they would do even greater things than Jesus had done. At Pentecost the Holy Spirit moved from filling the disciples to filling each member of the church. Acts 2:3 says, "And there appeared to them tongues as of fire distributing themselves, and they rested on each one of them" (NAS). The flame of the Holy Spirit rested on each one, changing forever the way God would relate to His children. Why is it hard to act boldly on this truth? Our claiming of the Holy Spirit should be just as natural for us as it was for the disciples, for He has empowered us, and He has clothed us with that very same power. In Matthew 28:19-20, we often overlook the fact that Jesus promised His presence and His power in the indwelling Spirit of God. This power is a personal power which comes from the Holy Spirit in our lives. It convicts, converts, renews, keeps, and comforts for the Christ Ones. This power is released in the Church. Its purpose is to equip the disciples to be witnesses unto the ends of the earth. Our response to the Holy Spirit should be to do what He has asked us to do.

God's Power Is God's Power

Evangelist Manley Beasley tells the story of a time he was very ill in the hospital. Several friends had come to cheer him up and to pray with him. While these men were praying for him in his room, writer and speaker Corrie Ten Boom walked in. Manley was hurting badly, but Corrie Ten Boom stayed several hours with him. Often, she would stand to her feet and begin talking to him, then all at once, the Lord would get her attention, and she would begin talking with Him. She would talk to Jesus a few minutes and then come back to Manley for a while. She was perfectly comfortable moving in and out of conversation with Jesus. Manley said that this fascinated him, and as he began to know this part of her life, he began to understand that she operated on the level of knowing Christ in an intimate way through His Holy Spirit.

Some years back, the Billy Graham Evangelistic Association expressed a desire to film a movie about Miss Ten Boom. Many months were spent praying over this film, and everyone came to the conclusion that it was the will of God to make it. About halfway through filming *The Hiding Place*, however, the Association called her with the dreaded words, "We're out of money."

"Oh," she said, "that is no problem. My Father owns the cattle on a thousand hills, and He will simply sell some cattle." She was so inhabited with the Holy Spirit that she already knew the will of her Father in this matter, and she acted on her faith. By the way, a rancher sold his cattle and his ranch and gave the proceeds to the Billy Graham Evangelistic Association. It happened just as she said it would. And the filming of *The Hiding Place* was resumed.

Because we know Christ and are indwelt with His presence, we can act on His power that is at work within us. Now, you may respond, "But, Esther, that's Corrie Ten Boom!" My response to you is, "That is the Holy Spirit empowering the life of a Christ One! God's power is God's power. It is exactly what He would like to do with you and me as we respond in faith and obedience to His Spirit within us."

"Do Not Quench the Spirit"

What is it that keeps us from responding and acting in the authority of the Holy Spirit? Let's look at 1 Thessalonians

5:19. Paul tells us, "Do not quench the Spirit" (NAS). Sometimes we think about the Holy Spirit only as an experience—and indeed, we do experience the Holy Spirit. But we need to remember that the Holy Spirit is also a person. He is part of the Triune God: God, the Father; God the Son; and God the Holy Spirit. When Satan knows the body of Christ is yielded to the Holy Spirit, he cannot penetrate that power. Satan's power is at work in our world. Just read your daily newspaper to see his activity. God's power in you is greater than Satan's power. You can go against Satan in the power of the Holy Spirit. Ask God, in the Holy Spirit's power, to bind Satan, to stop his activity in events, in circumstances, and in your life.

There is fear associated with the Holy Spirit. We are fearful of what other people might think when we talk about the Holy Spirit. We are afraid that the Holy Spirit might ask us to do something we do not wish to do. But remember, He is our Friend. He loves us. He empowers us. He illuminates us. That means the Holy Spirit gives light for us to follow, for He is in us. He illuminates Who He is in us. He directs us. He protects us. He guides us. The Holy Spirit equips us. We do not ever need to fear the Holy Spirit, but we are often afraid of what the Holy Spirit will do in our lives.

In addition, we sometimes believe that the Holy Spirit is just for deluxe Christians, or super Christians. However, all Christians experience communion with the Holy Spirit when they believe God for it.

I often hear about exciting things that are happening in the lives of other people. I used to ask, "Lord, why not me? Why can't I be filled with the Holy Spirit like Corrie Ten Boom or some other person that I know?" I've since come to the realization that this is because I haven't asked, and therefore, I haven't acted, on the faith that the Holy Spirit indwells me and clothes Himself with me. I feel much more comfortable if I can delegate this to superstars and people whom I know are super saints in Jesus Christ. But this isn't true! The Bible says the Holy Spirit comes upon us when we accept Jesus

17

Christ as our personal Saviour. We don't ask; and therefore, we don't act in faith like the book of Acts tells us to act. The men and women who were filled with the Holy Spirit at Pentecost went about doing marvelous things in the Father's name because they believed, and they acted on the belief that the Holy Spirit had filled them.

In his delightful book, *My Utmost for His Highest*, Oswald Chambers says, "The voice of the Spirit is as gentle as a zephyr, so gentle that unless you are living in perfect communion with God, you never hear it."[1] The Holy Spirit often comes as a still, small voice, so small that unless we are listening, we never notice it. Think about the noise-infested world in which we live. We are rarely quiet enough to listen to the Spirit of God. In the busy, fast-paced life we live, unless we take time daily to ask for power from the Holy Spirit and to listen to the Holy Spirit's voice, we will never know what the Holy Spirit could do in our lives. It is then easy for us to say that just those "special saints" know what it is like to have the Spirit of God in their lives. Not true! He has clothed us, as He did Gideon, and the Spirit of God will work through our lives, too. But we must be still enough to listen. Busyness is one of the greatest deterrents to the Spirit of God working in the lives of Christians today. We are so busy that we do not take time to invoke the presence of God and to know what the Spirit would speak to us. The noise and clatter we create shuts all of that out.

The Holy Spirit speaks to individuals every day. But, are we listening? Here are some things that might prevent your listening to the Holy Spirit. You might want to make a checklist of things in your own life.

• We don't follow through. We feel God leading us. He gives us a nudge. But then. . . nothing. This quenches the Spirit. I have done this in my own life. When the Spirit of God nudged me and told me to make contact with a neighbor, I kept putting it off and putting it off. One day my neighbor came to my door—to ask for help in lifting a bike from her car trunk to her garage. It gave me my first opportunity to

share with her who Jesus Christ was in my life.
• We compromise.
• We criticize others.
• We don't recognize the Holy Spirit because we depend on ourselves. How busy we are: our schedules to keep, our lists to do. How can the Holy Spirit work when we are depending upon ourselves?
• We are angry. Anger keeps us from having deep communion with the Spirit and from having *Koinonia* (fellowship) with the God of the Universe.
• We don't like ourselves. We often have our own "pity parties." Have you ever noticed that no one ever comes to that party but you? We need to look at ourselves as God's ultimate workmanship in His kingdom. Paul said that God's power is perfected in weakness.
• We're too busy. We don't wait before the Lord. We want instant communion on our timetables. The special person in your life right now, whether it be a spouse or friend, would be deeply offended if we gave the kind of time to him or her that we give to the Holy Spirit.
• We think impure thoughts. We give Satan an opportunity to work in our lives through our thoughts.

We need to live expectantly of what the Holy Spirit is going to do in our lives. He will put on our hearts the message He wants us to speak to the world in which we live. God is in this! Stop right now and write this down: **God's Holy Spirit is within me.** And we are within Him. Jesus told us in John 14:16-18 that He would be with us and God would be within us. He promised never to leave us alone. You see, He walks through life with us. He is our Companion. He cares about us: what we eat, what we wear, where we go, everything about us. If I ask the Holy Spirit, who dwells within me, to go with me to lunch, to committee meetings, to my exercise class, to everything I do, He does just that. We are the tabernacles of God. He dwells within each of us. He wishes to take our ordinary days and ordinary circumstances and put His supernatural power into our lives. Act on it! Faith it!

Joy in Surrender

Ephesians 3:19 says that in His presence is the fullness of joy. God desires that we "know the love of Christ which surpasses knowledge, that you may be filled up to all of the fulness of God" (NAS). He wants that to happen in our lives, and the only way it's going to happen is through the power of the Holy Spirit. So what is the secret of the Holy Spirit's incoming?

Every child of God has received the gift of the Holy Spirit. The secret is to **yield** and **surrender**. If my life isn't abundant in Him, it is not that He has not come in, but that I have not surrendered to Him who is already in.

Jesus said abide in me and I in you. Abide means to stay, to remain in a place where you already are. The believer is the sanctuary, the "holy place" where the Spirit abides.

How can I possibly experience the fullness of joy and the power of the Holy Spirit in my life when I struggle with self-esteem, comparing myself to others, and knowing I don't measure up? In that instance, my eyes are on myself, and I'm saying "I'm not," or "I can't." My focus is me, me, me, me. What I need to do is change my thoughts to Him, Him, Him, Him. The power of the Holy Spirit is within me! Of course, I'm going to fail and make mistakes. I am not perfect. But God's power can lift us above our humanity. We need to act in **faith**. It is not based on feelings. It is based on our convictions of God's truth. God's power lifts us above our feelings. God's power lifts us above our failures. God's power lifts us above earthly perspectives. So often, we become bogged down with the world in which we live. We need to remember that this world is not our home!

When Stephen was stoned, he looked to Jesus, not his circumstances. As he was being stoned, he was lifted into the presence of the Holy Spirit. By himself, he never could have said, "Father, forgive them." But through the power of the Holy Spirit, that is exactly what he asked God to do. When we are empowered by the Holy Spirit, He abides in us, and we abide in Him. We have a choice: We can live in our own power, or we can live in the power of the Holy Spirit. If we choose to live in the power of the Holy Spirit, then we discover hope in place of despair, courage in place of fear, power in place of weakness, and love in place of hate.

The Holy Spirit indwelling us can cause us to do incredible things. It can cause us to realize, like Moses, that we are on holy ground. It can blind us, as it did Paul, and give us a single vision for the rest of our lives. We need to pray with the Psalmist in Psalm 80:7, that His face will shine upon us and that we may be saved. The meaning of the ordinary things turned around by the supernatural touch of a Holy God will become extraordinary.

First John 2:1 says, "My little children, I am writing these things to you that you may not sin. And if anyone sins, we have an Advocate with the Father, Jesus Christ the righteous" (NAS). The One Who walks beside us is the Holy Spirit. He's called to stand beside us. Now, look at verse 6: "The one who says he abides in Him ought himself to walk in the same manner as He walked" (NAS). We are to walk the way He walked, and to do the work He has called us to do.

Ephesians 3:19 says we are to be filled with the Spirit to all fullness. The story is told that several pastors met to discuss inviting noted evangelist D.L. Moody to be the speaker for a crusade. After one man highly suggested Dr. Moody, another said, "It sounds like D.L. Moody has a monopoly on the Holy Spirit."

"Oh no," the first speaker replied, "Dr. Moody doesn't have a monopoly on the Holy Spirit. The Holy Spirit has a monopoly on Dr. Moody!"

Notes
[1]Oswald Chambers, *My Utmost for His Highest* (Westwood, New Jersey: Barbour and Company, 1963), 226.

Reflect Upon

1. God is the Father.
   God is the Son.

God is the Holy Spirit.

Which of the three do you feel most comfortable talking to? Why?

2. What do you perceive in your own life quenches the Holy Spirit?

3. Review chapter 1 and read all Scripture references again. Ask the Holy Spirit to reveal His truth to you as you read and to enable you to remember what He says.

Dear Holy Spirit,

I pray that I will live this day clothed by God. Come upon me and dress Yourself with me. As we walk together, do Your work through me. Amen.

2

Relying on the Holy Spirit as the Source of Power

In Matthew 1:23 we read, " 'The virgin will be with child and will give birth to a son, and they will call him Immanuel'— which means, 'God with us' " (NIV). The book of Matthew opens with an announcement that God will be with us. Then, at the end of Matthew, Jesus announces that all authority in heaven and on earth has been given to Him, and as we go, we are to make disciples of all nations. The book ends with the same promise: "Lo, I am with you always, even to the end of the age" (Matt. 28:20b NAS).

Jesus promised His disciples that they would be filled with the Holy Spirit. He told them He was going to leave someone with them Who would do greater things in them than He was able to do. That person is the Holy Spirit.

Total Dependence

I had an experience in January 1989 that taught me many good things about my relationship with the Heavenly Father.

My son, David, was serving in Vail, Colorado, as a semester missionary. My husband, Bob, and I had a speaking engagement in California, so we worked our schedules to stop by Vail and visit David for a few days. David had mentioned to me several times, "Mom, you really should try skiing! It is really super out here. This is *the* place to ski." Of course, I told myself that I could not do it because I had a very busy spring schedule, and if something happened to me, it would not be a good thing. I gave David several excuses as to why I couldn't. But when I arrived in Vail and got settled in, everyone looked so good in their ski clothes. It was snowing, and I guess there was a part of me that really wanted to ski. David kept saying, "Mom, you're an athlete! Come on, you can do it!" So I tried.

After skiing two wonderful hours on the "bunny slope," we moved up one level—and I fell and broke my right arm, a clean break! The Ski Patrol carried me down the slopes to the hospital. After the doctor set my arm, he told me, "You are out of business for a few months."

As I boarded the plane in Denver to fly back to Atlanta, Georgia, I began to learn a completely different life-style, sleeping sitting up and having someone feed me. I was totally dependent upon someone else for even the simplest things in my life—things that I had taken for granted. My husband had to dress me, undress me, bathe me, cut up my food, try to do my hair, and put on my panty hose! There was so little I could do for myself, for my right arm was attached to my waist in a body wrap. Moving from that tight system to a sling brought even more problems which I had to confront.

Now, I am a rather independent person, and I was raised in a home where if you were sick, you stayed quiet and did not ask for attention. As you might imagine, it was very difficult for me to have someone taking care of my every need. And the most disgusting thing about the whole affair was that Bob was taking care of me in such a gentle, kind way. If just once he had acted upset, angry, tired, or discouraged, I think it would have been a bit easier for me. Every morning, he would light a fire in the fireplace, and after coffee and devotions, he would go down to his office and leave me with my Bible, devotional books, and coffee. I would sit in front of the fire which gave me warmth and brought healing to my soul. Nothing can compare to the time I spent before the Father with His Love Letter open before my heart. I did several things during this time. I walked through the Bible and found all of the promises God had given to me in my life's journey and where He had given them. He showed me all of the places He had taken me as He walked before me. I would look up at the clock, and it would be 11:30 A.M. Hours had passed!

In this time, stillness came into my life. I began to sort out some things, and the Holy Spirit spoke to me clearly. Someone suggested that I read the book of Isaiah and as I came upon the word *Israel*, change the word to *Esther*. Doing this brought new understanding to me that I am the "new Israel."

Still, it was a long, painful experience learning to use my arm again. Just about the time I thought I could not stand it any longer, Bob would fix a candlelight dinner, and I would be overwhelmed again by the kindness, care, and love that he would give me. In fact, it was learning absolute dependence on another person to be my hands and feet that taught me something about depending on the Holy Spirit.

One evening, several weeks after the accident, I was preparing for bed—as much as I could prepare myself! Bob was assisting me, and he bent down to take off my tennis shoes. I was getting a bit more mobile, and I informed him, "I can do this by myself!" He looked up at me, smiled, and said, "But you don't have to." Much later I realized that the Holy Spirit wants my life to be as totally dependent on Him indwelling me as my physical life was dependent upon my husband during those weeks when I could do nothing for myself. Then I allow the Holy Spirit to clothe me and walk with me through my life. When He gave us the promises, "Immanuel, God with us!" and "Lo, I am with you always," He really intended for us to trust them!

During my recovery, I discovered another thing: when I

did begin to exercise my arm, I found that I had lost the use of all the muscles in it! It felt like a dead weight. When I didn't use it, I lost control of it. Perhaps this isn't the best illustration of the Holy Spirit, but when I have this power available to me and I do not use it, then it is of no value to me, and it becomes useless. As I began to build back my arm muscles, painfully stretching them—almost more painful than the accident itself—I began to improve little by little. My progress was based on my discipline to do the exercises faithfully and regularly. I began feeling so much better.

Then I got to where I could do most things for myself, and I let go of the discipline of my exercise program. Isn't that just like our relationship with the Holy Spirit? God's power begins to work in our lives, and we see what He does, and the next thing we do is strike out on our own. With my arm, I would have to back up and say to Bob, "Force me to exercise today! Don't let me get through this day without exercising!" Why? So my arm could become useful again.

Total Surrender

Let's look at what it means to rely on the Holy Spirit as the Source of our power. To rely on Him means we trust Him or depend on Him. Trust means surrender, and in surrender is obedience. Surrender, which is the supreme act of obedience, marks the beginning of a habit, a life of obedience to the Holy Spirit as I learn to yield myself to Him. Immediately, as I asked Jesus Christ into my heart as my personal Saviour, the Holy Spirit entered my life. It was not something that came later. I did not surrender my life to Christ in order to have the Spirit enter my life, but I surrendered my life to Christ because the Spirit entered my life.

The Spirit's presence in us is the promise of Jesus to us. Our response should be to continue to surrender our lives to Him and allow the Spirit to work through us. As we trust Him, He works. The Holy Spirit does not wish to have our plans, but our lives, so that He may work in us. It is one thing to work for God. It is quite another thing to realize that God works through us.

Did you ever hear someone say, "She is so full of the Spirit of God," as if the person speaking was not? Remember that the Holy Spirit in you is God's seal or promise that you are His. In Ephesians 5:18, the instructions for us are to continue being filled with the Holy Spirit. Filling us with the Holy Spirit is God's way of nurturing, growing, and equipping us for His service. The sad part is that so many of us accept Jesus Christ as Saviour, but we never allow the Holy Spirit to help us grow. We never move to the point of yielding or surrendering our lives to Him so that we can continue to grow and be equipped as saints to do the work of Christ in our world.

Sometimes it frightens us to think about the fullness of the Spirit when really, we are talking about yielding and surrendering. When you yield to someone, you give away, you move back, you stand aside, or you simply get out of the way. When you do that, you give the person to whom you are yielding an opportunity to go in front of you, and you follow. What a beautiful word picture of what the Holy Spirit does through us. When we receive the Holy Spirit, if we do not move aside and yield to Him, then we go about life without His power.

No wonder Christians often feel powerless! They are disobedient Christians who have not yielded to the Holy Spirit within them. It seems rather humorous to me that when we get into trouble, we cry out to God for help. Instead of crying out, perhaps we should cry within, because that is where the Spirit of God is—within us.

Oswald Chambers wrote, "Is my ear so keen to hear the tiniest whisper of the Spirit that I know what I should do? 'Grieve not the Holy Spirit.' He does not come with a voice like thunder; His voice is so gentle that it is easy to ignore it. The one thing that keeps the conscience sensitive to Him is the continual habit of being open to God on the inside."[1]

I must yield to the Holy Spirit inside of me! As I do so, then Galatians 5:22-23 will be the result. We are known by the fruit in our lives, and this passage teaches us that these fruits are love, joy, peace, patience, kindness, goodness, faithfulness, gentleness, and self-control. The Holy Spirit will reproduce these fruits in us, and they will make a difference in the world in which we live. As the Holy Spirit reproduces these fruits in my life, I will be His hands and His voice in my world.

Total Acceptance

Perhaps we do not trust the Holy Spirit in our lives because we have not accepted who we are in Christ Jesus. Let's look at who we are in Christ Jesus, which is who we are in the Holy Spirit. Read Ephesians 1:1-14. Then, underline the phrases *in Him* or *in Christ*. What I want us to capture is who we are in Christ Jesus, which is going to help us understand who we are in the Holy Spirit.

Allow me to walk through these verses with you. Paul addresses us as "saints," or holy ones. I don't know how being called a saint makes you feel, but it gives me goosebumps! We are holy ones.

Then Paul says, "Blessed be the God and Father of our Lord Jesus Christ, who has blessed us with every spiritual blessing in the heavenly places in Christ" (Eph. 1:3 NAS). Imagine that! Every blessing that He has is available to us! What we must do is make ourselves available. To me, this means everything that is His is ours (or at least is available to us)! In other words, because the Holy Spirit clothes Himself with us, all of His gifts are available to us. He does not give us His strength—He is our strength. He does not give us His hope—He is our hope. He does not give us His joy—He is our joy. Every spiritual blessing belongs to us—as children of God.

Paul continues, "Just as He chose us in Him before the foundation of the world, that we should be holy and blameless before Him" (Eph. 1:4 NAS). He chose us! We all want to be chosen. Paul reminds us that Jesus chose us in Him before the foundation of the world. We are chosen. We have acceptance in Christ Jesus.

Do you struggle with this concept? I know I do. We have a hard time accepting ourselves, so it is very difficult for us to comprehend that someone else has chosen us and accepted us. But that is exactly what Jesus did.

God accepts me, and that is God's grace.
I accept that He accepts me, and that is faith.
I accept me, and that is God's peace.
Now that frees me to accept you, and that is God's love.
And that, in turn, frees you to accept me, and that is God's fellowship.

What a wonderful truth to know that God accepts us. He chose us in Him before the foundation of the earth, and He has given us every spiritual blessing in the heavenly places in Christ Jesus. He has given us all the blessings that belong to Him.

In Ephesians 1:4, Paul tells us we are holy. We are holy ones. We are set apart to God. He adopted us as sons and daughters through Jesus Christ. We are heirs to His kingdom. (see verse 5). Have you ever intentionally done something good for someone? You were probably so excited about it. You anticipated it, you planned it, and it brought you such joy in doing it. The Father adopted us and made us sons and daughters in Christ Jesus because He intended to do just that, to the praise and glory of His grace which He freely bestowed on us in the Beloved. Therefore, we are to give Him our praise and glory. Ephesians 1:7 says, "In Him, we have redemption" (NAS). Through His blood, He bought us back. He redeemed us.

The Holy Spirit is a seal of what Jesus Christ did for us in redemption. A seal signifies ownership. Long ago a wax seal signified who owned the message being sent. The Holy Spirit is Christ's seal of ownership on us. He has sealed us and put a stamp on us that says, "This child belongs to the King! This is a kingdom citizen! This is a joint-heir with Christ Jesus! This person has every blessing available to Him through Jesus

Christ because I am sealing Him with My Holy Spirit!" What a promise! He pledged that we are God's own possession. Now, knowing all of these things, how can I not celebrate and rely on the Holy Spirit as a source of power in my life? He has given me all of these things in Christ Jesus, and He then says, "Esther, I'm going to take my ring, my seal, and I'm going to place it on your life. Do you feel it, Esther? Right there, sealed, My child. And in My child is the power of the Holy Spirit."

Total Power

In John 14:16-17, 26, Jesus said, "And I will ask the Father, and He will give you another Helper, that He may be with you forever; that is, the Spirit of truth, whom the world cannot receive, because it does not behold Him or know Him, but you know Him because He abides with you, and will be in you. . . . But the Helper, the Holy Spirit, whom the Father will send in My name, He will teach you all things, and bring to your remembrance all that I said to you" (NAS). We have a helper in the Holy Spirit whom the Father has sent. He has put this Helper within us, and that's what empowers us. John says that the role of the Spirit is to teach us all things and to help us remember all that Jesus Christ said.

I think of the Holy Spirit as my helper, and I rely on Him. I go in His power and His authority. Claim that verse right now as you learn to rely on the Holy Spirit. Pray now; ask the Holy Spirit to help you **rely** on Him.

Let's look at our theme Scripture Ephesians 3:20 in a new way.

Now to Him.
Now to Him who is.
Now to Him who is able.
Now to Him who is able to do.
Now to Him who is able to do exceeding abundantly beyond.

"Now to Him who is able to do exceeding abundantly beyond all that we ask or think, according to the power that works within us" (Eph. 3:20 NAS).

We could begin by saying, "Now to Him," and leave it with that. If we left everything to Him, we would not even need to finish the verse. "Now to Him who is." Who is what? Who is God. Who is the Holy Spirit. Who is the Son. There is enough power in those words for us to do all things.

"Now to Him who is able to do exceeding abundantly beyond anything we ask or think, according to the power that works within us" (Eph. 3:20 NAS).

I know what He can do through me. He can do more than I ask for, think of, or imagine. His power is at work within me. What I need to remember in this verse is the phrase "according to the power"—or His power—"that works within us." That's what we have to claim! We have to claim His power at work within us.

There have been times when I have tried to do everything by myself. So often, I get geared up, I get my lists made, I get everything organized, and I say I can do it all. Then, the Father brings me back to the place where I once again discover His faithfulness to me. When He calls me to do something, He says He will do it through my life. I become His hands, His voice, His heart, and His feet to do His work.

A short while back, my husband and I made a rather traumatic decision. We decided he would change from being on the staff of a local church to being a full-time free-lance composer/clinician. This meant that for a while, we would be living on one salary instead of two. This experience has been rather fun, kind of like being newlyweds again. We truly have relied on the Heavenly Father for everything in our lives.

One day in mid-December, I was in my car on my way to a doctor's appointment. Bob had been kind of discouraged; things on his calendar didn't seem to be falling into place, and the end of the month was quickly approaching. I did something then that I shouldn't have done. I let his discouragement get to me. As I drove to my doctor's office that morning, I talked to the Spirit about our situation, "OK, Holy Spirit, this is Esther again. My husband's discouraged today, and I need to ask You to provide for us. We need Your help." At that moment, the cassette tape in the car switched to a beautiful choral arrangement of Psalm 121. Those great words came soaring from the speakers, "I will lift my eyes to the hills—where does my help come from? My help comes from the Lord, the Maker of heaven and earth. He will not let your foot slip—He who watches over you will not slumber; indeed, he who watches over Israel will neither slumber nor sleep" (Psalm 121:1-3 NIV).

I cried out, "Oh God, if you are awake today, and I believe You are not asleep, that You are watching over us, then oh God, our Helper, look after our future." And then, as you might guess, through my tears, I sang all the way to the doctor's office along with the symphony chorus. I sang with all of my heart, believing and calling on the Helper.

After I completed my visit to the doctor, I headed home, feeling a peace inside me. I could not wait to tell Bob the promise that the Father had given me that day from the words of that great song. I began to share it with him. I said, "Bob, I asked God today to give us one thing to help us trust that He will help us in the future." At that very moment, the telephone rang, and I heard Bob say, "Yes, let me see. I'll check my calendar. Yes, I have that date open. Why certainly $400 is acceptable for what you are asking me to do." When he hung up the telephone, we stood up and danced around each other and sang and let the tears flow down our faces. Then we bowed our hearts and our heads to thank the Helper. That day, as we relied on Him, He showed us His promise that He is our Helper, and that He never sleeps nor slumbers.

One summer, I had a wonderful experience at Glorieta Baptist Conference Center, during Home Missions Week, teaching a witnessing seminar to a group of women from all over the western part of the US. One day, I closed the session with a story about Mildred McWhorter, a home missionary in Houston, Texas. Mildred is one of my favorite missionaries. She is full of the Spirit of God, and she lives empowered by the Holy Spirit. I shared a story with the women about a little boy who had come to the Baptist Center in Houston. Mildred had watched over him all week, and at the end of the week, he asked her, "Missus, are you God?"

Mildred was taken aback and said, "No." Then she asked herself how could she tell him who God is. She answered him, "God's love is in my heart."

He pointed up to her and said, "No, Missus, you're God."

Once again, Mildred tried to explain, "No, I'm not God, but God's love lives inside of my heart."

Again he said, "No." And pointing to her heart, he continued, "Oh no. You're God, and I can see Him right there." And that's true. We are the image of God to others.

The week ended. Then one of the women in that seminar ministered to me. She wrote a love note to me, sharing with me what the Father had taught her from His Word as we had met together. On the back of the envelope, which, of course, I saw first, she had written, "I know you're not God, but you sure are wearing His clothes!" My first reaction was, "Oh no! Oh no! Not me!" But my next reaction was, "Oh yes! Oh yes! Me!" If He indeed clothes Himself in me, then I must be wearing His clothes.

Notes
[1]Oswald Chambers, *My Utmost for His Highest* (Westwood, New Jersey: Barbour and Company, 1963), 134.

Reflect Upon

1. Have you accepted who you are in Christ Jesus? Galatians 2:20 says the Christian life is an exchanged life. "I am crucified with Christ: nevertheless I live; yet not I, but Christ liveth in me" (KJV). What may be keeping you from total acceptance?

2. Are you asking God for something He has already given you, that is, His Holy Spirit? Are you relying on Him? In what ways do you need His power today?

3. Reread each Scripture verse in this chapter. Pray, asking the Holy Spirit to reveal His truth to you as you read. You will remember what He says!

Father, Son, and Holy Spirit,

Teach me to stop asking for Your Holy Spirit's presence and help me to rely on the Spirit's presence within me. Teach me, God, to act on Your power in me. Amen.

3

Reclaiming the Meaning
of Missions

Sometime ago, I read with great interest Frank Tillapaugh's book, *Unleashing the Church*. In it Tillapaugh says that if we do not win America to Jesus Christ in the next decade ("we" being the evangelical church in America), it will be because of the "fortress" mindset of evangelical churches. The fortress mindset, he says, "is that we come inside the fortress to train for our mission strategy."[1]

Southern Baptists have done this well. We have developed several very good church programs. But a subtle thing has happened in our churches. Most everything we do in the name of Christ we do within the walls of the church. Tillapaugh argues that to win the world to Jesus Christ, we must unleash the church in the world. The church should be God's host is a hostile world.[2] We must penetrate the culture with the Gospel. However, it appears that we have developed our programs too well. We beg folks to come inside the sanctuary to our programs. Perhaps we have said *sanctuary* so long that we think of it as a place to hide, rather than a place to meet the face of God and be empowered by His Holy Spirit.

Having just read the book of Acts, I was stunned to see the fervor, boldness, and braveness of the disciples as they spread the story of Jesus Christ from Jerusalem to Judea and on to Europe. Notice in Acts the close connection between the disciples being filled with the Spirit and boldly proclaiming the gospel. So bold were they, in fact, that they were willing to give their lives for the cause.

Is that what the Holy Spirit requires? Our lives are so full of us and not the Holy Spirit. No wonder we don't act in boldness. Boldness cannot come from within us; it comes from the empowering of the Holy Spirit in us.

When a body of believers comes together, we worship and celebrate the Father. I fear sometimes we stop at that point. Instead, our worship should lead us outside the walls of the church into the marketplaces of life.

Where is today's salt and light in the community? Has the church become a part of the culture rather than standing against the culture? Has the church lost its place to stand because of its silence? Perhaps we need to reclaim the passion for the Great Commission. Today, God desires that we rid ourselves of the stereotypes of missions we may hold and think of ourselves as people called of God in the authority and power of the Holy Spirit to be salt and light in the world. That is His commission to us.

Reclaiming the Call

My life was changed forever at the joint Home Mission Board—Foreign Mission Board Commissioning Service held at the Centennial Celebration of Woman's Missionary Union in 1988. The celebration was held in Richmond, Virginia. Foreign Mission Board exective director of public relations Bill O'Brien and I were emcees. At one point in the program, Bill and I were to turn on miniature flashlights, like candles. Then we were to instruct people in the audience to turn on their lights to signify sending the light around the world. That night God let me see the stroke of His economy, His work in the world. First, retired missionaries from the United States and around the world paraded around the coliseum with their lights. Next, furloughing missionaries circled the coliseum. Then, the newly appointed missionaries made their way into the coliseum with their lights on.

I stood on the platform spellbound as I identified eight of those new missionaries—home and foreign—who walked in front of me. They had been my students when I had served as Baptist Student Union director at Samford University in Birmingham, Alabama. God had allowed me the privilege of walking with them on part of their journey, and here they were that night being commissioned to go around the world. In God's great economy, I had been a part of that journey— my prayers, my service, my life. How humbling and yet how awesome a privilege that experience was.

In that same service, newly appointed missionary Debra Owens-Hughes shared her testimony. She said, "With the recent celebration of Mother's Day, I've been reminded of my mother's great influence upon my accepting Christ's call to foreign missions. In March 1961 Myrtice Owens was speaking at the North Carolina WMU convention after her first tour as a missionary nurse in Tanzania. When she finished speaking, Miriam Robertson, then the North Carolina WMU state president, brought Myrtice's five-week-old daughter to present to the WMU. Well, here I am 27 years later being presented once again to the WMU. But this time, I am going to be commissioned as a foreign missionary. . . . And, now, just as my mother did, I would like to present to you my own daughter." Then Debra's husband placed their young daughter in her arms.

My heart cried, "Oh God, give us thousands of young men and women like Debra and her husband who are willing to give their lives and to offer the lives of their children, who are willing to claim the meaning of God's mission and call in their lives to live out the Great Commission in our world." For some, God's mission is indeed to be traditional missionaries around the world. For others the claim is to live out His call where they already are and to support those who go elsewhere.

I came away from the Centennial Celebration overwhelmed. The Holy Spirit nudged me to look at my selfish life-style. I was convicted by the fact that I often just glanced at a listing of missionaries on their birthdays and prayed, "God, bless all the missionaries." God's Spirit began speaking to me about altering my life-style in such a way that not only would I have "hands-on" experience with missions in my community, but that I would change my giving and my praying habits to make a difference in the kingdom of God.

When Christians work together, God gets His work done through His power in our lives. I'm not totally responsible for every person. What God has called me to do is to be obedient and responsible to His call, to be "on mission" as I go. We can touch people's lives if I am obedient in the place where God has placed me, you are obedient in the place where God has placed you, and that person over there is obedient in the place where God has placed her. Then, the Holy Spirit will "network" between our lives. I realized in Richmond, Virginia, that I wasn't the only person who had touched the lives of the missionaries who were commissioned. Parents, Girls in Action leaders, Acteens leaders, pastors, Sunday School teachers, Royal Ambassador leaders, BSU directors—God used all these different people to touch their lives. That means as these young missionaries go to serve around the world, part of me goes with them. And if you touched their lives, part of you goes with them. See how the Holy Spirit works? It is exciting! Surely I would become discouraged if I thought I was the only person God was using in someone's life. But no, God's economy is greater than that. He allows me to have a part in His mission, but others contribute, also. We work together.

Reclaiming the Power

The Holy Spirit seemed to claim the year 1988 to speak to me about the meaning of missions in my life and to reclaim that call to missions. That same summer, I attended the WMU Annual Meeting in San Antonio, Texas. At the close of the meeting one night, missionaries and program people left the convention center, got into boats, and started down the San Antonio River while holding miniature flashlights. Off to the side someone sang, "Send the light, the blessed Gospel light, Let it shine from shore to shore" (*Baptist Hymnal*, 1975). Bob and I were standing by a rail overlooking the river. A man was standing just in front of us. I knew he was a missionary because his name tag identified him as such. He was waving and shouting to the people, "Pray for us! Pray for us! You are our only hope. You are our last hope. Pray for us!" The Holy Spirit spoke to me again. He said, "Esther, learn what I asked you to do in Richmond. I asked you to pray for missionaries as you have never prayed for them before."

When God called me to follow Him as a young woman, I never felt that He was calling me to the missions field as a traditional missionary. But I have always felt that God called me to missions. Rereading the book of Acts affirmed this. In Acts it wasn't just the "professional" people that God turned loose to do His work in the world. No, it was all of the people of God: fishermen, tax collectors, business women, tent-makers, anyone who followed Him.

I was also in San Antonio in 1988 for the Texas WMU Annual Meeting. In one of the sessions there, we celebrated the 100th birthday of the Lottie Moon Christmas Offering. Flags of every nation where Southern Baptists work were paraded into the sanctuary. I stood with others and felt a sense of pride about what God has done through Southern Baptists. We are the largest mission-sending agency in the evangelical world. As each nation's name was called, the flag from that nation appeared. Then, black flags began to appear in the aisles. I was puzzled, and, by the whispers around me, I sensed others were puzzled, too. We watched in silence as these black flags were paraded down the aisle and to the front. A voice spoke these words, "The black flags represent the nations and people groups that are presently **closed** or **hostile** to the gospel of Jesus Christ." I stood ashamed. I was stunned. As I stood there, God's Holy Spirit reminded me that I am a part of His plan to go into all of the world. Silently, through my tears, I again prayed for God to change my praying, my giving, and my going.

Reclaiming the meaning of missions is having faith in the Holy Spirit to empower us to make disciples in our world. It is not just a structure, although God does use structures. It is not just a program, although God does use programs. It is not just an institution, although God does use institutions. Perhaps we need to reread the account in Acts and see what happened to His disciples.

First of all in Acts 2:14-39, we find Peter preaching in the power of the Holy Spirit. Three thousand people responded to his message that day. Acts 2:43 says everyone kept feeling a sense of awe, and many wonders and signs were taking place through the apostles. Not long after that, Peter healed a lame man. In Acts 4 Peter and John were jailed—but not before the number of new believers had risen to 5,000. Peter, full of the Holy Spirit, preached Jesus Christ before their accusers: "If we are being questioned today about the good deed done to the lame man and how he was healed, then you should all know, and all the people of Israel should know, that this man stands here before you completely well through the power of the name of Jesus Christ of Nazareth—whom you crucified and whom God raised from death" (Acts 4:9-10 TEV).

In verse 13, their accusers recognized them as having been with Jesus. The disciples could not stop telling what had happened to them. How long has it been since someone said about you or your church, "Why they've been with Jesus. I can tell." Later in chapter 4 the Bible says the believers were one in mind and heart. They shared everything with each other. No one claimed his belongings for himself. No wonder the community said about them, "Look how they love one another." Can you imagine what would happen if we, who claim to know the power of the Holy Spirit in our lives, took everything we have and laid it at the feet of the Lord?

Reclaiming Stewardship

I can hear you asking, "Esther, do you want me to sell everything I have and give it away?" Would you consider doing that? Nothing actually belongs to you, does it? When you accepted Christ into your life, you gave up the right to ownership.

Culture tells us we are what we own—our identity comes from what we have. Jesus taught stewardship, not ownership. He said to concentrate not on what we own but on what we can give away. Remember his encounter with the rich young ruler in Matthew 19?

Consider these thoughts:

• I make my home available to God. I invite friends to break bread and to discover the Bread of Life.

• I lay my car at His feet—to carry meals to the homebound and people to the doctor's office or grocery store.

• I lay my goods at His feet. When I purchase a new dress, book, or compact disk, I give one away so I won't hoard.

• I lay my office at His feet. I allow Him to empower me as I share Jesus Christ in my work place.

• I lay my children at His feet. They are His gift to me. If He takes them to the ends of the earth, He goes with them, and so do I through love and prayer.

• I lay my money at His feet. No, not 10 percent—it's all His. I am a steward. I am just as responsible for what I do with the other 90 percent.

Stop and look at His resources in your hands. Pray, asking the Holy Spirit to teach you what to do with His resources.

Discovering our Marketplaces

As you continue reading in Acts, you will discover even greater works of the Holy Spirit in the lives of the believers. Many believers were persecuted and jailed; Stephen was even stoned to death. Still, God's followers remained faithful to Him and allowed Him to work through them.

Ananias was one such faithful follower. In Acts 9 the Holy Spirit instructed Ananias to visit Paul, "But the Lord said to him, 'Go, for he is a chosen instrument of Mine, to bear My name before the Gentiles and kings and the sons of Israel" (Acts 9:15 NAS). Don't you know Ananais was afraid! But Ananias was obedient. He went to Paul and discovered that the Holy Spirit had changed his life.

Now put yourself in Ananias' place. Has the Spirit of God instructed you to go to someone you know? to a stranger? to another group of people in our nation? to another people group in our world?

As I read Acts, it occurred to me that all who believed immediately turned to tell someone about Jesus. They took the gospel to the sick, to the well, to the jailers, to the authorities, to all of the world. From Acts we can see how the Word of God spread from nation to people group to nation. That's exactly what the Holy Spirit is asking us to do today. He's asking us to discover our marketplace and to reclaim the meaning of missions. Missions is every Christian's responsibility. Can you imagine what would happen in our world if each Christian, empowered by the Holy Spirit, allowed God to claim his life?

There is much emphasis today on "marketplace missions," that is, the people of God taking the message of God into their work places. This is not a new idea. Paul made his living making tents, and as he did so, he proclaimed the good news of Jesus Christ. Where is your marketplace? Where do you go each day to make a living? Have you thought of that as your missions field? Think of the places you visit each day or week: the beauty shop, post office, grocery store, office building, hospital, doctor's office, bus or subway, bank, gas station, repair shop, day-care center. Can you make a difference for Christ in those places?

I challenge you to develop a "Thank You, God, it's Monday" concept. Do not dread the start of a work week. Instead, consider it the starting point for serving Christ that week. Think of the work week as the time when the church—the body of Christ—is scattered and going about His business. On Sundays, He brings us back together to worship Him and report to each other what the Spirit of God did through us in our marketplace missions fields that week. I can't think of anything that would turn Bold Mission Thrust around faster in Southern Baptist life than if you and I began to think of Monday as the start of our marketplace missions fields.

My marketplace is often an airplane, traveling from one engagement to another. Somedays, it is my office or MARTA, Atlanta's rapid transit system. Each week I pray, "Thank You, God, that I have this week to be on mission in the world!" Stop now and pray. Ask the Holy Spirit to show you your marketplaces and to make you obedient in them. Make a list of your marketplaces, and pray for persons in each area.

Sylvia lives in Boston. Her husband, Don, owns a shoeshine concession in Logan International Airport. Don considers himself to be a "light in the ghetto." He happens to have his shop at the busiest spot in Logan Airport. As people walk down the concourse, his stand is immediately in front of them. Someone asked him one day how he got that location. Don replied, "God gave it to us. God put us here, and we are going to give it back to God."

In her testimony, Sylvia says, "People don't have much respect for shoeshine people. I am a college graduate, but God has given me the opportunity to touch people at the crossroads of life. When I think that Jesus Himself was willing to wash people's feet, I thank Him for the privilege of shining shoes." Sylvia leaves her business every afternoon, goes home, takes off her business suit, and puts on jeans and an apron. She goes to the airport to relieve Don, so he can have a break. She bends down and shines shoes.

She says, "You know, ordinary people don't get their shoes shined. Extraordinary people do: rich folks, famous folks, show business folks, professional athletes, politicians. Our shoeshine stand is an opportunity for Don and me to touch base with people that we would never have an opportunity to witness to in any other place. You must be quick to tell people about

Jesus in the shoeshine stand. We place a Bible on our stand, and people usually ask us about it. We keep tracts that we give away to people. Very often, we just say, 'We'd like to pray for you. How can we pray for you in your life?'

"We're kind of like hairdressers. Folks will come in and dump on us all the problems they won't tell anyone else. They tell us about their kids and problems at home, and we try to comfort them through Jesus Christ. We ask if we can pray for them. We share the message of salvation, and we talk about the name that is above every other name—Jesus. God has placed us there in that stand to share His good news."

Sylvia says, "if Christians do nothing, the Gospel will be little-known and less understood, so we've got to do something. We are ambassadors for Christ! People see us as nonpersons, in coveralls and plastic gloves. But what they don't know is that Don and I are ambassadors for the King. He has called us, saved us, and given us a holy calling, and He has empowered us with His Spirit to be His ambassador on our knees—shining shoes." That, friends, is reclaiming the meaning of missions in the marketplace.

Ken, a Florida pastor, began a program in his church to meet needs in the community. On Sunday afternoons, people gather at the church then go out to work in different ministries. One group buys groceries and cooks dinner for the local Salvation Army shelter. They serve the meal and give out New Testaments. Another group in his church visits the local children's hospital. They visit the children and their parents and minister to them in any way they can. Linda, a nurse in the church, participates in this ministry. One Sunday afternoon, she visited a ten-year-old boy and his father. The father was a pastor in the area. During the visit, he said to Linda, "This is Sunday; shouldn't you be in church?" Linda said, "Sir, this is church."

Scott is a lawyer who does negotiations for professional athletes. He also visits a local hospital regularly to minister to people who are dying of Acquired Immune Deficiency (AIDS).

A leading heart transplant physician in the Southeast who is a member of Ken's church is involved in a jail ministry. He goes to four different jails and holds worship services for inmates. Recently, after four consecutive visits, 120 inmates made professions of faith.

Another group in Ken's church ministers in a Veteran's Administration hospital. They take cookies to families of patients, visit with them, and take them to dinner or give them a ticket for a complimentary meal at a local cafe.

Each Sunday evening, all groups meet at a local restaurant to tell one another what the Holy Spirit did in their ministries that afternoon.

Reclaiming the Mission of the Church

In the book *A Whack on the Side of the Head,* Roger von Oech challenges us to look at situations and problems upside down to get a different perspective.[3] It works; try it. Mentally, stand on your head and look at the church in your neighborhood. Pretend you are not a Christian. How would you want the church to "mission" you? What could that church do to impact the community and world?

Jesus told His disciples that after He ascended, He would send forth the Holy Spirit, and the Holy Spirit would look after the affairs of both individuals and the world. Acts 10:34 says that "God is no respecter of persons" (KJV). Sometimes we get in our little corners and think God is working only in "our corner" or in "our denomination" or through "our convention" and that God will only work according to "our precedent." The Holy Spirit can't be bound by time and space.

God says He will pour out His Spirit "upon all flesh" (Joel 2:28 KJV). Remember that as the Lord ascended, the last thing the disciples saw of Jesus was His pierced hands. This same Jesus will come back again. This same Jesus said to His disciples, "I have to go away. . . so that I can leave the Holy Spirit with you, because you are going to do greater works than I have done because the Holy Spirit will be with you."

Imagine that, Jesus trusted those 12 disciples to carry on the work of His kingdom. He is now trusting us to do so, too.

It is exciting to see the Holy Spirit at work. As I travel about this country, working through my denomination, I meet men, women, and teenagers inside and outside my denomination who are acting on the power of the Holy Spirit. It is evident that the Holy Spirit is empowering them for what they are doing. I find myself celebrating this. The Spirit of God works across denominational and local church lines. The Holy Spirit can work anywhere He wants to. He is not the resource for a particular church, denomination, or religious group. Instead, the church is the resource for the Holy Spirit in the world. And who makes up the church? The people of God.

Several years ago, I paraphrased Matthew 25 for a song in a musical. The song, titled, "When, Lord" goes like this:

The King is coming in all His glory,
To gather the people of every nation around Him.
Some will sit at His right hand; some will sit at His left.
To those on His right, He will say:
"Come on in, you're welcome. Come on in and share my kingdom.
Come on in and spend eternity with me eternally,
For I was hungry, and you fed me; I was thirsty, and you gave me drink.
I was naked and you gave me your clothes. I was sick and you took care of my needs.
I was in prison and you paid my bail. Come on in, you're welcome!"
"When, Lord, when did we do these things for you?"
"When you fed the hungry, that was me.
When you helped the hurting, that was me.
When you clothed each other in my care, that was me.
You do it all for me!"
(To those on His left, He will say:)
"Depart, now! My kingdom is not yours.

Walk away, now. You did not see the least of these;
So why should you see me?"
"Why, Lord, are we not welcome? Why, Lord, is Your
kingdom not for us?"
"You chose not to feed me, as you ignored the hungry.
You chose not to visit me, as you neglected strangers.
You chose not to clothe me, as you wrapped up warm
yourself.
You chose not to heal me, as you overlooked my pain.
You chose not to love me, as you loved those already loved."

Does this text describe any local church bodies today who
are so busy looking after themselves that they do not see the
hungry, the imprisoned, the hurting? Have they insulated
themselves inside the walls of their own fortresses? The Holy
Spirit is asking us to release His power in us to minister to
the hungry, the illiterate, the disenfranchised, the refugees,
the strangers. Child of God, that is exactly what it means to
reclaim the meaning of missions.

Can you imagine what would happen in our world if each
Christ One, empowered by the Holy Spirit, reclaimed God's
call in their lives?

Notes
[1]Frank R. Tillapaugh, *Unleashing the Church* (Ventura, California: Regal Books, 1985), 8.
[2]*Ibid.*, 8-9.
[3]Roger von Oech, *A Whack on the Side of the Head* (New York: Warner Books, 1983).

Reflect Upon

1. Jesus said, "When you feed the hungry, that is Me. When
you clothe each other in My name, that is Me." What have
you done in His name?

2. Where is your fortress? List the things you do inside your fortress. Make another list of things you do outside the fortress.

3. Look at your church from a different perspective, perhaps as a non-Christian or as a new resident in the community. How does it appear to you? Does anything need to be changed? What could you do to make your church more appealing to people outside it?

4. Reread each Scripture passage in this chapter. Ask the Holy Spirit to reveal His truth to you as you read. Pray that you will remember what He says.

Dear Holy Spirit,

Make me so uncomfortable as I sit inside my fortress that I will be willing to be a part of Your mission in Your world. I pray that my hands will become Your hands, my lips will become Your lips, and my walk will become Your walk. Help me to understand that as I go, I am Christ in my world. Amen.

4

Recognizing and Providing
Entry Points
for Personal Involvement

During the reign of Oliver Cromwell, the British government began to run low on silver coins. Lord Cromwell sent his men to the local cathedrals to see if they could find any precious metals. The men reported, "The only silver we could find was the statues of the saints standing in the corners," to which the radical soldier and statesman of England replied, "Good. We'll melt down the saints and put them into circulation."

Just imagine—melted saints, circulating through the mainstream of humanity bringing worth and value to everyday life. Not dressed up, polished, three-piece-suit, briefcase-in-hand, shiny-silk-dress saints, comfortable on a padded pew on Sundays. No, Jesus wants us to be melted down saints in the marketplaces of life—on campuses, in shops, in corporate offices, in homes, on the streets—everywhere people are. We are not to be statues in the church shiny and polished, but we are to melt into society as saints empowered by the Holy Spirit.

One summer several years ago, my husband was invited by

Walt Disney World to direct the "Kids of the Kingdom" in the College Workshop Program. While there he learned that every afternoon in Disney World or Disneyland there is a parade. Employees in both places are expected to don costumes or performance outfits and march in the parade. He was told that one day a man stopped Walt Disney and asked him, "Why do you have a parade every day?"

Walt Disney answered him, "When you march in the parade you see the eyes of the people watching the parade, and you remember why we have a parade."

God sent his son, Jesus Christ, to march in the parade of life. From the New Testament it is clear that everywhere Jesus went, He marched with a purpose and intent that was given Him by God. Everything Jesus did pointed to God, the Father. Likewise, everything the Holy Spirit does in our lives points to God.

Crossing Barriers

We, too, must intentionally cross barriers to reclaim cities and villages in our land for Christ. Have you considered making deliberate choices in order to evangelize and minister? Jesus did just that in John 4. On his way to Galilee, Jesus passed through Samaria. The usual route to Galilee was to go around Samaria, because Samaritans were considered undesirable people. Jesus chose to go straight through Samaria. He stopped by Jacob's well, just outside the city of Sychar, for water. He encountered a woman, and He stopped to visit with her. In His encounter with the woman, Jesus crossed several barriers. The first barrier crossed was sex: He was a man, she was a woman. In those days a man did not converse with an unaccompanied woman. The second barrier He crossed was their religion. He was Jewish, she was Samaritan. The Jewish people did not have any use for the Samaritan people. They were outcasts in society. The third barrier Jesus crossed was her reputation. The woman was divorced and living with a man to whom she was not married.

The woman had come to the well to draw water. Jesus knew that her thirst was not only physical but spiritual also. He told her about the living water that is available to all who ask. He introduced Himself to her and said, "I am He. I am the Messiah."

There are people everywhere waiting to hear about the living water: in Chicago, New York City, Boise, Charleston, Miami, Houston, San Fransisco, Phoenix, Jakarta, Hong Kong, Rio de Janiero, Nairobi, Paris. They are waiting for you and me, who have the living water within us, to tell them about it, too.

Perhaps we need to follow the example of Ray, from Chicago. He and his family deliberately chose to live in a racially mixed neighborhood that is marked by violence. On their block alone, 17 nations are represented. In the school system of 470,000 students 53 nations are represented. Forty percent of students come from single parent homes. Over one-half are ethnics. Ray says that he and his family purposely chose to live in the community to be a witness for Jesus.

Deliberately choosing where to live is one entry point for personal missions involvement. An entry point is an opportunity we find to share Christ with others. Christ asks us to penetrate our culture with the gospel. He wants us to be in the world, but not of the world. Consider what might happen if Christians chose neighborhoods, schools, and workplaces with the intent of sharing the gospel instead of on the basis of earning power.

I was intrigued by a 79-year-old woman I met one summer. When I met Carmen, she was serving as a house mother for college-age summer missionaries in Daytona Beach, Florida. I asked Carmen why she had volunteered for work at age 79.

"Esther," she said, "it all started when I was 64 years old. I read an article in *Royal Service* urging Christians of any age or circumstance to go as Christ commanded. As I read the article, I tried to decide where I could go. The Lord began to speak to me through this article, and I opened my Bible and sought His direction. He first led me to Genesis 12:1: 'The

Lord said to Abraham, "Leave your country, your people and your father's household and go to the land I will show you' " (NIV). Then He led me to Jeremiah 8:20: 'The harvest is past, the summer has ended, and we are not saved' (NIV). The next verse in my devotion was Lamentations 1:12: 'Is it nothing to you, all you who pass by? Look around and see' " (NIV).

Carmen decided she was too old to be on a payroll, but she was not too old to work. "I felt called, and that feeling has never left me. I know it's true, for I couldn't do what I do if I didn't feel called." She has since worked in missions in Arizona, Pennsylvania, and Florida.

"Carmen," I said, "you live in Georgia. What do you do with your house while you are gone on these missions appointments?"

Carmen smiled and said, "I just lock it up and say, 'Here it is, Lord. Take care of it 'til I get back! You told me to go.' " Carmen recognizes there is a place for her to be involved in her world. She said, "I have never said no to anything God has asked me to do."

Ethel is another person who has found her entry point in missions. One Wednesday night at prayer meeting, the Lord told her she needed to go to a certain family in the community and take food and money. When she arrived at the home she found the family in tears. The mother was ill, and all their money had been spent on medical bills. There was none left for gas or food. The family had just finished praying for God to send help. Ethel was the help that God sent to this family. The Holy Spirit spoke to her to go, and she was obedient. She said to me, "I was the person God needed to answer someone else's prayer, and that alone is reason enough to listen to the Holy Spirit."

After attending a national evangelistic meeting for women, I received a letter from Shelby, one of the conference attendees. She wanted to share with me some of the things she had learned at the meeting and how God had already led her to use them. Several days after returning home from the conference, a friend called Shelby to talk about a situation in her life. Shelby took the opportunity to share Jesus with her friend.

That same day another friend called Shelby. This friend had been widowed at a young age and was struggling to raise two young boys by herself. She was now in a relationship with a man but did not feel the relationship was right for her. Shelby realized her friend needed a fresh insight from the Word of God. She said, "Since I had just returned from a place where He was fresh and new to me, I was able to let the Holy Spirit love this friend through me. I had felt the Holy Spirit nudge me before to speak to this friend about this relationship in her life, but I had not been bold enough to do that. What I learned is that in my business for the Lord, I had just about lost sight of who I am in Him. I learned again that I have to have His boldness, and I need to be obedient and share His Word."

For Shelby, her entry point into missions involvement was her telephone. She was open to God using her to minister to others, and He led them to her by way of her phone.

The Little Things That Really Count

I met Kay in Atlanta several years ago, and I have discovered she really does live by Ephesians 3:20. Kay resides in an upper-middle-class suburb of Atlanta and is involved in the youth ministry in her church. At Christmastime the youth minister wanted to involve the youth in a ministry project. Kay volunteered to ask a downtown women's shelter if the youth could do something for the shelter's residents.

The youth decided they would invite the women and their children to attend a performance of the church's special Christmas music program. The youth would provide transportation to the church and back and would fix lunch for the persons attending. Kay made the arrangements for the youth.

For most of the youth, this was their first contact with the homeless. Kay recalls, "It was a freezing day, about 18 degrees. We had a nice meal, enjoyed the service, gave presents to our guests, and then returned the people to the shelter." When they arrived at the shelter, however, the doors were still locked. It had not yet opened. The last persons off the bus were a woman with two small children and a three-week-old infant. Kay said to her husband, "We can't let them off in this cold." Turning to the woman, she asked, "If we let you off, where will you go?" The woman answered, "I'll just wander the streets until the shelter opens." Kay and her husband banged on the doors of the shelter until someone came and agreed to let the family in early.

Kay continued to think about the family. She said, "The Lord just touched me. I had never seen or felt anything like this before. I went home thinking, it is almost Christmas and these people are living on the streets all day long—even with a baby." She asked her family, "How would you like to invite the mother and her children to spend Christmas with us?" Members of her family agreed they wanted to do that, so Kay contacted the family at the shelter and made arrangements for them to spend Christmas day with Kay's family.

When Kay went to pick up the woman and children, the woman asked her if they could also include the woman's husband. Kay asked, "You mean you have a husband, and you live in this shelter?"

The woman explained, "Yes, but my husband lives in the men's shelter. We can't stay together."

Kay agreed, and after picking up the husband, they went by the hospital to check on the baby who had become ill. At the hospital, they discovered the baby was well enough to be released, but the doctor did not want to release her to go back to the shelter. As the family stood there trying to decide what to do, Kay thought to herself, I do not know these people. But aloud, she said, "They can all stay at my house."

Kay discovered that the family had come to Atlanta from Missouri to look for better jobs and a better way of life. They had lived in a trailer for a few months, but after the birth of their third child, they had been evicted because the trailer park allowed only four persons per unit. From there they had gone to the downtown shelters.

The husband had been looking for work, but thus far had had no offers. Kay realized the couple were a lot like her, except that they had married early in life, had no formal education past high school, and had had a lot of obstacles to overcome. Kay offered to keep the children in her home while the couple looked for work. So for two weeks, during Christmas vacation, the homeless family became their extended family.

Before long the husband found a job. A member of Kay's church provided them with a rent-free apartment until the family could get back on their feet financially. Other members provided furniture, clothing for the children, and food for the pantry. When Kay returned to the shelter to pick up the family's belongings, the director expressed thankfulness for what Kay's family had done. Kay told her, "We haven't done much—not compared to you and your staff. You're the ones who work here seven nights a week providing a place for these people to stay. We've really done very little."

The director responded, "If all churches would do just a little, we could take care of the homeless in Atlanta. It's the little things that really count."

After this experience, Kay quit her full-time job and began working part-time. She started doing volunteer work at the women's shelter one day a week. She also became involved in a ministry in her church that provided care to persons in need. The ministry needed someone to interview persons who came for help in order to assess their needs. Kay became that person. Other persons in Kay's church were prompted by her example to become involved in helping meet needs. Kay found a downtown soup kitchen that needed help, and several church members began serving there. After a while, the church's Baptist Women organization took over coordination of the soup kitchen.

Brenda was Kay's friend. While on a prayer retreat Brenda was asked this question: "What are you doing to make a difference in your world?" Brenda said she had never thought about that before. "All my life, all I've done is be a mother and play tennis. I was so involved with myself!" she explained.

The question kept nagging at her heart. She decided she needed to do something to make a difference, and so she set up a job bank where people who lacked skills in job hunting could come for help.

Brenda learned that many job hunters lacked education or skills. Many lacked transportation, and most lacked child care. These were just a few of the obstacles displaced people face. Through the job bank ministry, church members coached persons on interviewing skills, drove them to interviews, provided care for children or sponsored the children at a day-care center, and helped match persons to jobs available.

Kay, Brenda, and others involved in these ministries learned that meeting physical needs of persons provided entry points to telling them about Jesus. Kay said, "These people have heard the Bible before, and many of them know it well. But until we are willing to get out in the pouring rain and move someone into an apartment, put groceries in their car, or stand beside them in their time of need, they won't see the love of God in our faces or actions. You don't quote Scripture to them when they are going through the line at the grocery store. As you stand beside them in line you are showing that you care enough to give your valuable time, and then they see God in you."

We are to be God's hands in day care, His justice in the job bank, His mercy in the car pool, His comfort in the shelter, His provision in the food lines, and His compassion in the streets. When we feed others, we are feeding Him. When we clothe others, we clothe Him. When we find them a job or home, we are doing that in His name. What an incredible opportunity the Father gives us as He clothes us in His power.

Networking

Charles is a pastor in Florida. His goal in life is to facilitate the laity of his church for ministry. One of the first ministries the church began was one to the homebound. Over 400 church members minister weekly to the needs of homebound persons.

In one year over 100 homebound persons made professions of faith in Christ as a result of this ministry.

Next, the church started a rescue mission for transients. The mission provides food, shelter, and clothing to persons in need. In one year, over 3,500 people were helped. Each week the church takes an offering over and above their tithe to be used in this ministry. One couple in the church volunteered to oversee the ministry, recognizing it as an opportunity for them to be God's care givers in their community. On occasions when the rescue mission is full, church members take transients into their homes. The church gets calls for help from all over the United States. Most people stay in the mission an average of two nights.

Sponsoring the rescue mission led the church to begin another ministry: providing temporary homes for the children of transients. Some members even became foster parents. Many of the children had never experienced living in a Christian home before.

Yet another ministry started by the church is an emergency pregnancy care center. The first 12 months the center was open over 1,100 women came for pregnancy testing, counseling, and childbirth classes. The ministry is not residential, but if a woman needs a place to stay during her pregnancy, church members make their own homes available.

Charles says, "All of what we do is 'networking.' One need leads us to another need, which leads us to another need." As they meet needs, members tell about the Person Who is behind all that they do: Jesus Christ.

A dark side to life in America is the abuse of women, children, and the elderly. I discovered this when I became a volunteer in a shelter for abused women. Many Christians have no concept of the hurt and fear that is prevalent in the world today. One church I know in the midwest has started a ministry to abused children.

In 1976 there were 170 convictions for child abuse in this midwestern city. By 1981 there were over 8,000. In cities across our nation statistics like these keep increasing. This city, as well as the church located there, became aware of this growing problem. Social workers in the community needed 4,000 volunteers to assist with the needs of abused children, but they were only able to secure 300. The local child abuse agency came to the church for help.

The agency asked the church for volunteers willing to spend two to three hours a day working with abused children. Volunteers would spend time with the children, play games with them, help them with homework, and be their friends. The church responded by saying, "We are Christians, and as we help these children with their homework and other things, we will want to share Jesus Christ with them."

The agency's response was, "We don't care. We want these children to receive love and guidance and support. If you want to share Christianity with them, then share it."

Most churches are "event" or "program" oriented. We promote programs from birth to old age. The event or program is the church's entry point for others. Our culture has come to expect that of churches. What our culture doesn't expect is for the church to go to the jails, to the high-rise apartment buildings, or to the shelters. We should not give up these wonderful programs in our churches. But we should look at the needs of society and develop strategies that will bring the church to the people.

Consider these opportunities:
• a Christian lawyer who works toward reconciliation rather than divorce, and shares about the reconciling love of God;
• a physician who not only helps his patients with their physical sickness but also helps them to understand their spiritual sickness as well;
• Christian school teachers who volunteer one afternoon a week to help illiterate adults learn how to read and write;
• professional workers tutoring international students at a local unversity. Many of these students come from countries that do not allow missionaries in. After graduation the students will return to their native countries to live, and they could take the gospel with them.

Child of God/Priest of God

We have relegated for too long the priestly role in the church to the paid clergy. Every child of God is called to be a priest before God. If God has not called us to be missionaries as our professions, then we can use our chosen professions or other skills we have as entry points for missions involvement. As we work we can recognize the needs of the world and make a difference in Christ's name. If we are to reclaim the meaning of missions, we must get outside the church and let missions become a way of life for us. Do you dare ask these questions of yourself: What are the gifts God has given me? What are the needs in my world? What can I do to make a difference?

Before we can discover God's direction for us, we must read His Word daily, because the Holy Spirit speaks to us through His Word. We must also develop sensitivity to the place where God has put us. For example, if you had told me a few years ago that I would discover entry points for missions on an airplane, I would have said, "No, not me!" Now, I spend a great deal of time on airplanes, and God gives me many opportunities to share Him with fellow travelers.

Frank Tillapaugh tells the story of a church in Boston that was packed every Sunday back in the 1940s. Next door to it was a cafe where a foreign exchange student worked to pay for college. The student's name was Ho Chi Minh, and he would one day become the ruler of Vietnam. Members of that church lost out on an opportunity to change the world.

Do you recognize places where God can use you in missions today? Consider these entry points:

• sponsoring support groups for alcohol and drug abusers and other persons experiencing problems;

• being a big sister or big brother to a child from a broken home;

• inviting several couples into your home for dinner and including a non-Christian couple;

• providing job counseling and training to unemployed persons;

• providing support and assistance to women with crisis pregnancies;
• tutoring latchkey children, thus giving them a safe place to wait for parents to arrive home;
• coaching or participating in a city sports league.

An Acteens organization traveled north one summer to conduct Big A Clubs for a week. A Big A Club is a way of teaching about Jesus to children who have had little contact with church. The weather was unusually chilly for that time of the year. One of the children who came to the Big A Club sat shivering. "Where's your jacket?" the Acteens asked.

"I don't have a jacket," the little girl replied.

The Acteens told their leader, "We've got to find a store and buy her a jacket!"

The leader thought to herself, they can't possibly afford to do that! She prayed, "God, what should I do?" As she drove down the road, she noticed a sign indicating a garage sale in progress. She pulled off the road, and the girls got out in search of a jacket. They found a jacket that needed just a little mending. That evening the Acteens mended the jacket, and the next day they lovingly presented it to the girl. Only then did the Acteens realize that the other children were shivering in the cold as well.

That night the Acteens plotted what they could do. They took some canvas tarp they had with them and cut it into triangles, making canvas shawls to wrap around the children for warmth. The Acteens realized they could not tell these children about the love of God while the children sat there shivering. Their physical need had to be met first before their spiritual need could be addressed. These Acteens recognized an entry point and became involved in meeting a need in Christ's name.

Can we do less?

Reflect Upon

1. What would it cost you to move from your secure neighborhood to be on mission in your city?

2. How can you penetrate the culture with the message of Christ from where you live?

3. Make a list of people in our society who might need help; for example, teenagers, financially poor, homeless, unemployed. Next to that list, make a list of your gifts and abilities. Ask the Holy Spirit to lead you to a ministry in a new area.

4. Read your local newspaper with the intent of discovering ministry opportunities. What did you find?

5. List entry points for missions involvement in your life. If you cannot think of any, pray that God will put some in your life.

_____

Father,

I'm feeling very uncomfortable right now. I wept most of the afternoon. My heart breaks over the hurt in my city. God, what were You thinking as I cried? Do You wonder, why the tears without any action? So do I. Amen.

5

Realizing the Diversity
of the World
and Risking Involvement

Jennie Robeson, a journeyman nurse in Ethiopia, said she was
overwhelmed by the needs in that country when she arrived.
She wasn't there very long before she began to question the
value of her contribution to the ministry. She learned a valuable
lesson from a 1985 *The Commission* magazine article. In the
article, Mary Saunders, a volunteer to Ethiopia at that time,
was quoted as saying, "I've lived in African villages and seen
pockets of hunger, but not the vastness of the need here. What
I do here feels like a drop in the bucket. But I remember the
Swahili proverb, 'drop by drop, the bucket fills.' "[1]

My father, now an 84-year-old retired Baptist minister,
taught me so much about our Heavenly Father. As a girl, I
would make my way from my room to the bathroom each
morning to prepare for that day. One morning, upon hearing
Daddy's voice, I walked across the hall to his study (in those
days, ministers had their studies in their homes). I understood
that this was where he met God. When I looked in the door
on that particular morning, I saw a scene that I have kept

inside my heart all these years. My father was on his knees, with his Bible open before him, and he was praying the Psalms back to his Heavenly Father.

About 8:30 every morning, my parents open God's Word and *Royal Service* and pray together for missionaries by name. Then they lift each of their 5 children, 12 grandchildren, and 3 great-grandchildren by name in prayer to God. I believe that my parents' prayers make a difference, even if it's just a drop at a time. What a risk we take when we join God through prayer in His work in the world. My parents kneel daily to offer their children, grandchildren, and great-grandchildren to the Father. What risk, you ask? The risk that God will call some of these children, or grandchildren, or great-grandchildren to minister thousands of miles away as missionaries. But they wouldn't have it any other way.

Risking Through Prayer

We risk with the Holy Spirit when we pray that His power will be released in the lives of the people for whom we pray. What an exciting risk we take as we become involved in a world that is so diverse. Imagine, my prayers can release God's power around the world. We are part of the work of God as we join the Spirit through intercession.

One missionary I interceed for is Dorothy Osborne. Dorothy and her husband, Darrell, serve in Nigeria. It is a thrill for me to pray for them because I have known them a long time. I baby-sat their children in Kamloops, British Columbia, when I was in high school. I remember when Dorothy and Darrell came to know Jesus Christ as their personal Saviour. It happened one Sunday night after my father's local radio broadcast. The phone rang after that evening's broadcast. It was Dr. Osborne. "I heard you speak tonight," he said, "and if you don't come to my house right now, my whole world will fall apart—my family, my marriage, my career. I need to talk with you." My father left immediately to visit the Osbornes, and that night he led them to accept Jesus Christ. Can you see God's economy? My father risked to be obedient in sharing Christ, and now the Osbornes serve as medical missionaries in Nigeria. The Holy Spirit worked through my father to release His power in Dorothy and Darrell.

We live in a very busy and diverse world. Yet Jesus said, "My kingdom is not of this world" (John 18:36 KJV). Oswald Chambers, in *My Utmost for His Highest*, wrote, "The great enemy to the Lord Jesus Christ in the present day is the conception of practical work that has not come from the New Testament, but from the systems of the world in which endless energy and activities are insisted upon, but no private life with God. The emphasis is put on the wrong thing. Jesus said, 'The kingdom of God cometh not with observation, for lo the kingdom of God is within you,' a hidden, obscure thing. An active Christian worker too often lives in the shop window. It is the innermost of the innermost that reveals the power of the life."[2]

The time I spend in the presence of God releases the power of the Holy Spirit, empowering me to risk involvement in my world. As I think about the risk, I am reminded of 1 John 4:4, "Greater is he that is in you, than he that is in the world" (KJV), and John 14:10, "The words I say to you are not just my own. Rather, it is the Father, living in me, who is doing his work" (NIV). The Holy Spirit's daily leadership is the defining characteristic of every disciple.

Let's look at some facts about our world:
• 5.1 billion people live on earth.
• 3.4 billion of them are not Christian.
• 1.3 billion (26 percent) have **never** been given the opportunity to respond to the Gospel.
• Society has become valueless. *USA Today* (11/27/89) called the 1980s the "Decade of Excess."
• 6 million women are beaten in their homes each year (one every 18 seconds).
• In 50 percent of these homes, the children are beaten as well.
• Teens spent $55 billion on themselves last year.
• 2 million Americans are addicted to cocaine.

- Today's children will see 100,000 beer commercials by age 18.
- Nearly 800 million adults cannot read or write.
- More "foreign" missionaries come to America than to any other country in the world.
- 41,000 children die every day because of hunger and hunger-related diseases.
- In the next 30 minutes. . .

29 teenagers will attempt suicide.

57 teenagers will run away from home.

14 teenaged girls will give birth to babies out of wedlock.

22 teenaged girls will have abortions.

When I read facts like these, I am overwhelmed. It will take risk to reach a world in crisis. I need the Holy Spirit to remind me that it can be done "drop by drop."

We live in a culture that says "Me! Me! Me! Find out who you are. Do what feels good. Live and let live." This is directly opposite to what the kingdom of God is about. Jesus said, "If you want to find your life, then give it away." How radical. What a risk: to die to self to make a difference in the world.

Multiplied Power

The Holy Spirit blew fresh on my life one morning as I read John 14. In this passage the disciples asked Jesus, "Show us the Father." Jesus responded, "How can you say, 'Show us the Father?' Don't you believe that I am in the Father, and that the Father is in me? The Words I say to you are not just my own. Rather, it is the Father, living in me, who is doing his work. Believe me when I say that I am in the Father and the Father is in me. . . . I tell you the truth, anyone who has faith in me will do what I have been doing" (John 14:9-12a NIV). I stopped reading right there. Did He really mean that if I believe in Him, I will do the work that He did? The second part of that verse answered my question: "(You) will do even greater things than these, because I am going to the Father" (John 14:12b NIV).

I continued reading, "And I will do whatever you ask in my name, so that the Son may bring glory to the Father. You may ask me for anything in my name, and I will do it. . . . And I will ask the Father, and he will give you another Counselor to be with you forever—the Spirit of truth. The world cannot accept him, because it neither sees him nor knows him. But you know him, for he lives with you and will be in you" (John 14:13-14, 16-17 NIV).

Jesus said the Holy Spirit would guide us even more than He could. That is because Jesus' ministry on earth was limited to where He could be physically. When Jesus left to go back to the Father, the Holy Spirit stayed with the believers. The Holy Spirit is not limited to one place physically. As believers fan out across the earth to spread the Gospel, they are about the business of the Great Commission, and the Holy Spirit guides and empowers them. The Holy Spirit is at work within each of us wherever we are. That's how He is going to get His work done: not only through those 12 disciples, but through His disciple Esther, His disciple Susan, His disciple Bill, His disciple (your name). If Jesus had not gone back to His Father, His ministry would have been local. Instead, He is multiplied through the power of His Holy Spirit in us around the world.

Jesus has called you and me to risk. When I read through the book of Acts and see what the disciples Paul, Barnabas, Timothy, Stephen, and Peter were willing to do, I wonder if I have sacrificed at all, or if I even know what it means to risk. Am I willing to go in my Father's Name, empowered by the Holy Spirit, to become involved in my world?

If the church in today's world is an indication of what the Holy Spirit is doing in the world, we might ask the question, "What on earth are we doing?" Southern Baptists have become a large, well-organized, and wealthy denomination. Yet we cannot organize the work of the Holy Spirit. We cannot buy what the Holy Spirit can do. What we can do is join the Holy Spirit in what He is already doing in our world. We can become a people before God, reclaiming the meaning of missions. We can join other Christians in our communities and around the world to reach the lost. It's risky, that's for sure. It may require us to give up ownership in order to have partnership.

Commitment—What Does It Mean?

Deborah Brunt, in *Contempo* magazine, gave this definition of commitment: "Commitment requires focus. When you're committed, every part of you is heading in the same direction."[3]

Mike Burczynski, pastor of Trinity Baptist Church, Moscow, Idaho, says that commitment is crucifixion. "The Lord Jesus was ever calling for this 'death to self' extreme." In following Christ to a small church in a pioneer missions area, Mike left a thriving church in the South and took a 60 percent pay cut. That sounds like a risk to me![4]

Jim Queen, home missionary to a racially mixed, inner-city community of Chicago, says, "(Commitment is) giving myself over to God completely to follow Him, to do whatever He says."[5] Jim moved into the inner city where the pimps, winos, and homosexuals live, because Jim believes that Jesus came for them, too.

R. G. Whitehead, home missionary in Arizona, says, "(Commitment is) being true to our God. Commitment really begins when we commit our lives to the Lord Jesus Christ. It means we would rather die than betray Him."[6]

According to Cooperative Services International worker Mike Stroope, "(Commitment is a) continual and radical redirection of life. (Its evidence is) values, life-style, and actions which result from constant examination and refocusing of life."[7]

I once heard Mike give his testimony. In it he said, "Pray for me and my family. My family will live in Europe, and I will commute to work in a country where my family cannot live. I will be risking, and it will be dangerous for me to be outside of the call of God."

As I heard Mike speak, I prayed, "Oh God, give us a thousand young men like Mike Stroope and his family who are willing to risk their lives. Give us thousands of young men and women who are willing to risk in order to go empowered by the Holy Spirit to make a difference in the world." Then I heard the Holy Spirit whisper to me, "I use 52-year-old women, too." Risking. . . in a diverse world.

Risk Takers

Lynn and Stan Steepleton are risk takers! They served in Oregon-Washington as US-2 missionaries, working with the hearing-impaired. When they finished their two-year term there, they returned to Birmingham, Alabama, to minister to the deaf at McElwain Baptist Church. I visited in their home once and was able to observe their family devotion one morning. Stan gathered their two young sons by a world map that hung on the wall. He opened the magazine *Royal Service* to the listing of missionaries on their birthdays, and said, "Boys, let's pray for the missionaries this morning." Each boy chose a missionary. Then they took little flags and pinned them to the map on the places where the missionaries serve. The family then bowed their heads and prayed for those missionaries.

I later said to Stan, "That really touched me."

Stan answered, "Esther, We're not only teaching our children to pray, we're also teaching them the theology of geography. We want them to understand that the world is a lot bigger than Birmingham, Alabama." In 1989 Stan and Lynn were commissioned as foreign missionaries to the hearing-impaired in the Dominican Republic. Lynn and Stan have realized the diversity of the world and are willing to risk.

Dot, an acquaintance of mine, risks involvement in her world in Atlanta, Georgia. Dot is an industrial nurse for a cosmetics manufacturer. Because of the power of the Holy Spirit in Dot's life, she is a daily witness to the people with whom she works. Dot has started a Bible study at work with co-workers. She is on mission in her marketplace.

A church in Washington, D. C., sponsors a group that serves as a "lobby" for Jesus. They do a thorough study of the lives of the politicians who serve our nation. From newspapers, magazines, and interviews, they try to discover what drives these political leaders, what principles they live by, and how they vote. The group is interested in people in the powerful places in Washington as well as across our nation. The members will show up on the steps of the Capitol to meet a particular leader. When this leader comes from the building the group will tell him courteously, "We want to meet you and let you know that we wish to pray for you. We want you to know we are interested in your work. We want to pray for your work as you represent us in our nation's Capitol."

In one encounter, the senator the group met cried. He was so pleased to know that he was not bearing his burdens alone but had people who cared enough to pray for him personally.

Think what would happen if Christians prayed daily for our political leaders—global, national, and local. The Spirit of God would be freed among those people in powerful places to do His work.

Darcy, a high school student, participated in a missions trip to Pennsylvania. The group planned to conduct a Big A Club in a community in that state. As they canvassed the neighborhood looking for children to invite to the Club, they met the mother of a mentally retarded child. The mother wanted her daughter to come to the Big A Club, too. The child was large and awkward. Darcy thought to herself, I really wish this child would not participate. But the next day the mother appeared at the Big A Club with her daughter. Darcy said the other teenagers kept passing around the responsibility of looking after this retarded girl. "You look after her." "No, you look after her." Finally, the group turned to Darcy and said, "You need to look after her." You see, Darcy has a younger brother who is retarded.

"I didn't want to do it, either," Darcy said. But all week, during the Big A Club meetings, Darcy befriended Nancy. They sat together, ate together, and did crafts together. "I really felt the Holy Spirit telling me that this is what I should be doing," said Darcy. "And when I became obedient to Him, it was a good experience for me."

When the week was over, Nancy said to Darcy, "You're the best friend I have in the whole world, and you may be pretty on the outside, but you're prettier on the inside." Risking. . . with someone who is different from you and being the love of God to that person. . . that's what Darcy did.

Would you risk and become a "tentmaker"? A tentmaker is someone who prepares for a career and intentionally plans to work overseas with an international company. The person works for this company, and they pay his or her salary, but he or she also deliberately penetrates that culture with the gospel of Jesus Christ. The person looks for opportunities to share Christ with the people there. Many foreign countries no longer allow missionaries in. But Christians can still reside in them through secular jobs.

Do you dare risk such a life-style?

For several years, my husband, Bob, took a group called the Baptist Festival Singers on a singing tour of Europe. This group sang concerts of sacred music in about five countries during a two-week tour. Almost every year, the group gave a concert in Interlaken, Switzerland, and stayed in the same hotel, The Swiss Chalet. The owner, Frau Schmidt, became our good friend. Each time we visited, we became a little better acquainted, and we had more opportunities to plant the seed of the gospel with her. She said to me one evening, "There is something different about your group. I have other groups who come to my chalet, but they just don't act like this group. Your group acts like they love each other. Could you tell me what the difference is with them?" That was our first entry point with her—why we were different from the other groups and who we were in Jesus Christ. One year the Singers went up the mountain to Grindelwald, a tiny ski community in the Swiss Alps, to sing in a worship service. I felt the Spirit of God nudging me to remain in the hotel with Frau Schmidt that day. I wasn't sure why. It wasn't long before Frau Schmidt informed me she was going to take her puppy on a walk around the lake and asked if I would like to go with her. I eagerly took her up on her offer. As we sat by the lake that afternoon, she began to share some of the struggles and loneliness in her life. For the first time, I had the opportunity to share Jesus Christ with her. Using a tract, I presented the plan of salvation to her and asked her if she would like to ask Jesus Christ to come into her life. She answered, "No, but Esther, pray for me, because I am feeling something inside of me." I trusted that it was the Holy Spirit working within her.

After we arrived home from the trip, I began to send her letters and cards, sharing with her who Jesus Christ was in my life.

One year later, the Baptist Festival Singers returned to Interlaken. We arrived at The Swiss Chalet, and as we got off our tour bus, Frau Schmidt ran up to me, embraced me, and said, "Esther! Esther! I found your friend, Jesus!"

"Tell me about it," I replied. Frau Schmidt explained how she had gone to a luncheon with a Christian business organization and had heard the Gospel presented once again. There she had accepted Jesus Christ into her life.

Risking. . . to share the gospel with someone who is different from me, who speaks a different language than I speak, who has a different background, and who comes from a different culture. Jesus Christ and the power of the Holy Spirit span all cultures and all peoples, and we are to go in the power of the Spirit to share this Saviour.

Would you risk becoming involved with the elderly people in your community? I recently read in a national newspaper that elderly people in America are called "the throwaways." The article said that many elderly people spend hours sitting in shopping malls because of loneliness.

I know of a church in the West that began ministering to senior citizens. They conducted Bible clubs and other activities for them. One of the women they became acquainted with was Ion. Ion was 89 years old. She did not have any relatives who visited her in the nursing home. Women and men came from the church to visit with her, and they discovered that Ion could play the piano. She used to play a piano in a bar, and she could play all kinds of music. The group began to minister to Ion on a regular basis. They helped her with her makeup, showing her a color chart and what "season" she was. They brought her food and remembered her birthday. At 91 years of age, Ion came to the Bible study and asked Jesus Christ to come into her life. At 92 she was baptized, and at 93 she went to be with her Heavenly Father. She had been one of the lost and forgotten elderly of our nation until someone risked to minister to her.

The Home Mission Board says that the largest group of people who volunteer for service today are adults, many of them retired. They are at a point in their lives where they no longer need to work, yet their health is good, and they still have many productive years ahead of them. Many work as Mission Service Corps or Christian Service Corps volunteers. Mission Service Corps is for long-term volunteers. Persons must provide their own salary, but if one is retired, that is no problem! Christian Service Corps is for short-term volunteers— usually less than one year. Again, the person must provide his own support.

Mae is one such retiree who is willing to risk. Mae took early retirement as a high school business teacher. At age 55 she volunteered in the Peace Corps for two years. After that she became a regular volunteer through the Foreign Mission Board. At least four to six months out of every year Mae is living somewhere overseas, fulfilling a short-term volunteer assignment for the Board.

The needs across our nation and world are many and varied. The retired have a lifetime of experience to draw on as well as the gifts God has given them to risk and become involved in the world. Do you dare risk in your retirement years to meet needs of others and help them come to know Christ?

Robert was raised in a hollow in Kentucky. His pastor helped him obtain a scholarship to attend Cumberland College, a Baptist college in Kentucky. Robert's roommate at Cumberland for a while was Steve, the son of a doctor. Over time the two roommates learned about one another and the diverse backgrounds from which each had come. One day Steve told Robert that he would like to see a "holler," so Robert took him to see Canada Town, a small community in one of the hollows named for the Canada family. Mr. Canada, his wife, and seven children all lived in that hollow, and several of the children had married and built homes of their own there. Steve was amazed at what he saw. These families were living in "slab houses"—one-room dwellings made from slab wood, with no running water, indoor plumbing, or windows. Most of the adults had little or no education. Few could read or write. And most families included six or seven children. Steve said, "We've got to do something!"

Robert and Steve risked. They began a program called "Mountain Outreach." They enlisted other college students to go into the hollows and help build better homes for the people who lived there. The homes were not elaborate—at that time they cost just $3,000—but they were adequate.

Robert is now a seminary graduate, serving in Alaska, but the Mountain Outreach program—building homes for folks in those Kentucky hollows—still continues.

At one time my job at the Home Mission Board included assigning youth groups for missions trips. I sent many youth groups to that Kentucky hollow to assist the college students in building homes and to conduct Big A Clubs. The teenagers worked alongside the college students pouring foundations, putting up dry wall, and doing all the other tasks involved in building a basic house. After one such trip, I asked a teenaged girl about her experience. "What did you think?" I asked. "How are you different because of your Kentucky experience?"

"Oh, Mrs. Burroughs," she began, "when I went there, I was worried about little things like chipping my nail polish. After I had been there a week, little things like that weren't important any more. I've never seen such poverty. It was so good for me to go there and to discover how much I have, in comparison to them."

I had the opportunity to visit Cumberland College one day, and I was anxious to meet Robert while I was there. I told him I wanted to visit Canada Town and see the work the volunteers had done. "Are you positive?" he asked. I told him yes.

That afternoon Robert took me to visit two homes in the Canada Town hollow. The first home we visited was Linda's. I'd never seen anything like it in my life before. She invited us into her home, and when I sat down on the couch, I almost went to the floor. My vision was in direct line of the kitchen table, which was a large wooden spool (the kind that telephone wire is stored on). The walls were bare except for artwork the children had brought home from school. Their beds which consisted of mattresses on the floor were neatly made. The entire house was clean and neat. And Linda was very proud of it. As we got up to leave, she reached out and touched my dress, and said, "You are so beautiful." She didn't mean me; she meant my life-style. Compared to her, I am rich.

Robert and I walked down the hill to visit Mary, Linda's sister-in-law. I could hear Mary yelling and screaming at her children when we were still some distance from the door. There were seven of them—running all over the house and each other. We entered the house and Mary said, "Sit down!" I sat down on the sofa, and this time I did go all the way to the floor—my knees came up to my chin! It was an uncomfortable position for me, but Robert wasn't uncomfortable. These were his friends. We visited a bit, and then Mary said, "Robert, I just can't get those math problems!"

Robert said, "Mary, I have trouble with them, too." Then I watched Robert bend over Mary's third-grade math paper and assist her with her homework. She was preparing for the GED test. What a risk taker. For a moment, I thought I saw Jesus. Indeed, I had in the life of Robert, who was empowered by the Holy Spirit with a passion to make a difference in his world.

As we returned to the car that day, I couldn't stand it any longer. The tears began to flow freely, and I said, "Oh Robert,

I had no idea that in my nation there was that kind of poverty! Thank you for what you have shown me today and for the Spirit of God I sense in you."

I could not wait to get home to tell my family about Canada Town. It changed our Christmas. Through my tears, I said, "We can't afford to do Christmas in this home like we did last year—not with the hurt that is in the world, especially in Canada Town." So instead of spending the money on presents for ourselves, we spent it on presents for the people in Canada Town. And it was a wonderful Christmas!

Sometime ago I read a story about a church in Nigeria. During a church service there, the deacons prepared to take an offering. A 12-year-old boy was sitting on the front row. He was well known to this congregation, for he was an orphan who had absolutely nothing. When the deacon passed by his row, the little boy stood and asked the deacon to stop. The deacon asked him, "Son, what do you want?"

The boy answered, "I want to give all that I have to Jesus."

The deacon said, "Sit down, Son. You have nothing to give. We know who you are."

But the little boy insisted, "All that I have, I want to give to Jesus tonight. Please lower the collection plate." The deacon lowered the plate to the floor. The boy stood, faced the congregation, and said, "I have nothing of what you have, but all that I have, I give today to Jesus." And with that, he sat on the collection plate. That's what the Holy Spirit wishes from you and me. That's what will enable us to risk in our diverse world. We must give all that we have to Jesus.

Acteens from a church in the southeast know how to risk. These girls wanted to do something to make a difference. They began a ministry to pregnant high school girls who live in a home for unwed pregnant teens. The Acteens began by inviting girls from the home out to dinner and other fun activities. Friendships began to form, and the girls from the home asked to come to Acteens every week. Next, they joined the church's youth group for Wednesday Bible study. The girls and the church's youth group sat together in worship services on Sunday morning—how risky for an upper middle class church. Barriers began to fall, and God's love was shown to these girls. In late summer the girls joined the church's Acteens and youth for a lock-in. That weekend, Tara, one of the girls from the home, asked Jesus to be her Saviour. Tara's background included drug use and street living. Her family did not want her. A few months later I sat in the worship service and watched as the youth minister baptised Tara. My son, David, sat by my side, and I leaned over and whispered to him, "The only difference between Tara's sin and mine is that hers shows and mine doesn't always." As tears rolled down my face, I thanked God for Acteens who were willing to risk through the power of the Holy Spirit.

Another risk taker is a church near Atlanta, Georgia. It adopted an entire low-income, drug- and crime-infested neighborhood in Atlanta. The neighborhood was in serious trouble. The church worked with city and community officials in providing services such as a job fair, a health fair, music and art events, sewing and reading groups, music and ballet classes, after-school tutoring, and classes for teens. As the church became active in the community, drug dealing and crime decreased. People in the community were no longer afraid to live there. A minister from the church was assigned as minister to the community, and his expenses were paid by the church. A new church was begun there.

Think what would happen to crime and other problems in our cities if other churches were willing to become involved in undesirable neighborhoods. Risky? Yes. Hard work? Very much so. Possible? Of course, through the power of the Holy Spirit.

The church in Atlanta was willing to go outside its walls—its fortress—to penetrate the culture with the gospel. How do we usually start churches? Oftentimes, we start a church by finding a place to meet and issuing a "you all come" invitation. This method may have worked well 20 or 30 years ago, but today's cities need alternatives. We can no longer put up a white-columned church with a steeple, hang out a sign, and expect people to come. The world has changed. The culture must see the church in the marketplaces and neighborhoods of life. It must see the Holy Spirit at work through Christians in all walks of life.

Jesus called the religious people in His day, "whitewashed sepulchers." He said they were a people that honored Him with their lips and not their lives. What would He say to the church today as we redecorate our sanctuaries and build bigger and better worship centers, yet do not give enough to meet the goals for our special offerings for home and foreign missions? Risk? Yes, it will take a risk for us to speak up and turn that trend around.

What is Jesus Christ's Address?

In the August 1989 issue of *The Commission* magazine, Foreign Mission Board president Keith Parks tells about visiting a shop in Ho Chi Minh City (formerly Saigon). In the shop Parks met a Vietnamese man who had visited several places in the United States in his training as a pilot. He had flown for the United States Air Force. After the fall of South Vietnam, the man had spent time in a Vietnamese Reeducation Camp. The man shared some of the circumstances of his life and the great desperation he felt to find a better life. He told Parks he was very poor. They had trouble communicating with each other, but Parks discovered that this man had never heard about Jesus Christ. He had lived in three different Southern states, yet he had never once been invited to a church. No one had ever told this man about Jesus Christ and his need for Him as personal Saviour.

Dr. Parks explains, "Trying to communicate in simple terms, I began describing the fact that his circumstances, which he had defined as being desperate and unsatisfactory, could be changed.

" 'I personally cannot help you,' I said. 'However, I know someone who can. His name is Jesus Christ.'

"Instantly, he responded, 'What is His address?' "

The question, "What is the address of Jesus Christ?" stunned Dr. Parks. "The obvious reality was like a kick in the stomach. The actual, practical address of Jesus Christ is every Christian."[8]

The everyday address of Jesus Christ *is* every Christian. Wherever we live, wherever we work, wherever we go, Jesus Christ is within us. He has called us to risk and to become involved in our diverse world.

Notes
[1]Robert O'Brien, "Viewing Africa: Ethiopia—Drop by Drop, Love Fills the Bucket," *The Commission* 48 (September 1985), 58.
[2]Oswald Chambers, *My Utmost for His Highest* (Westwood, New Jersey: Barbour and Company, 1963), 293.
[3]Deborah Price Brunt, "Commitment: Counting the Cost," *Contempo* 19 (July 1989), 7.
[4]*Ibid.*
[5]*Ibid.*
[6]*Ibid.*
[7]*Ibid.*,8
[8]R. Keith Parks, "What Is Jesus' Address?" *The Commission* 52 (August 1989), 79.

Reflect Upon

1. How do you feel about risking? What might have to change in your life in order for you to take a risk in Christ's name?

2. Is it foolish to talk about risk and being empowered by the Holy Spirit in the same conversation?

3. If Jesus' address is every Christian, when was the last time someone asked you for His address? What would you say if someone asked you that question?

My child, I've often heard your question: This message is my answer.

You're concerned about the hungry in the world, millions who are starving . . . and you ask, "What can I do?" **FEED ONE**

You grieve for all the unborn children murdered every day . . . and you ask: "What can I do?" **SAVE ONE**

You're haunted by the homeless poor who wander city streets . . . and you ask: "What can I do?" **SHELTER ONE**

You feel compassion for those who suffer pain, sorrow and despair . . . and you ask: "What can I do?" **COMFORT ONE**

Your heart goes out to the lonely, the abused and the imprisoned . . . and you ask: "What can I do?" **LOVE ONE**

Remember this, my child . . . two thousand years ago the world was filled with those in need, just as it is today, and when the helpless and the hopeless called to Me for mercy, I sent a Saviour . . . **HOPE BEGAN WITH ONLY ONE!**—B. J. Hoff

6

Renewing in the Spirit
Through Prayer

Empowered by the Holy Spirit to live a Spirit-directed life. . .
. . . to bow your heart toward God in prayer
. . . to bend your life in surrender to God
. . . to be obedient to the Spirit in your walk.

Time spent every day with God in prayer and in His word allows the Holy Spirit to empower us, so that we may increasingly become persons wholly filled and flooded with God Himself and able to risk in our world. This happens only by spending quality time in His presence. Doesn't that sound simple! It's not, however. It is a discipline, and when it becomes a part of your life, you will discover that you can't live without it! You will feel such a "oneness" with the Spirit of God as you bend your heart in prayer before Him and as you ask Him to speak to you through His Word.

Centering on God

As I prepare for whatever God asks me to do, I first ask the Holy Spirit to speak to me through His Word. I ask for God's direction, and always, the Holy Spirit speaks, although it may not be in my time frame. He gives me fresh insights into the Word of God. Praying in the Spirit means using the power given to us by God to maintain a Spirit-directed life. What God desires is our "oneness" with Him. He is in us, and He wants us to be at one with Him.

Recently, I attended a family reunion with my four brothers and sisters to celebrate Father's Day. It was the first time in over 30 years that all of our family had been together at one time. We experienced a wonderful weekend full of talking, laughing, crying, remembering, and praying. At the end of the weekend, I went for a walk with my older sister, a beautiful Spirit-filled woman with a Spirit-directed life. I said to her, "This has been so good, but what I really need is to get home and get off by myself and think through some of the things we've said. I'm feeling a bit homesick for God right now." I had been caught up in four days of constantly being with family, for we hadn't seen each other in such a long time. Yes, we opened God's Word and prayed each morning as a family, but that wasn't my time alone with the Heavenly Father. I felt "homesick," a longing to be still before God.

The Quakers call this action "centering." Gordon Mac-Donald refers to it as "ordering your private world," which is the title of a book he wrote on the subject. When we come before God in prayer and meditation, we "center" in that innermost being where the Holy Spirit speaks and works through us. We make a place for God. To be empowered people of God, we must bend our hearts toward God in prayer and give the Holy Spirit an opportunity from within us to fill us.

This filling happens most often in a quiet place. Think of the busy world in which we live. . . the fast pace at which we travel. . . the diversity in our lives. Yet our Heavenly Father reminds us that we must bend our hearts before Him. Perhaps from time to time, we should bend our knees before Him, too. I don't think the position is as important as the practice, however. T. W. Hunt, LIFE Consultant for Prayer in the Discipleship Training Department of the Baptist Sunday School Board, says, "Prayer is work. . . but prayer works."

If it is true that our prayers release the power of God in the world, no matter how diverse the world is, then there is real power in prayer—and *every* believer has that power!

When we pray in the Holy Spirit, He already knows our needs. In fact, you met the Holy Spirit before you knew Him or knew who He was. He convicted you. That voice within brought you to a relationship with Jesus Christ. What He is asking of us now in an empowered life is to walk with Him, to abide with Him. God can supply everything we need. I believe He puts the needs in our lives so that we must depend on His supply. Then, He can show us Who He is. Matthew 6:7-8 says, "And when you pray, do not keep on babbling like the pagans, for they think they will be heard because of their many words. Do not be like them, for your Father knows what you need before you ask him" (NIV). If I think I have all that I need, I will not rely on the Holy Spirit. If we go in our own strength, we will run out. But if we go in His strength, we do not run out.

One sign of the Holy Spirit within us is when we realize that we are empty, we come before Him knowing that He can fill us with His Spirit.

Henry Blackaby, director of Prayer and Spiritual Awakening for the Home Mission Board, says, "In prayer before God, what happens is we adjust our lives so that we will come in harmony with all the resources and activity of God. If I go into my work place to figure out what I am going to do or what my church is going to do, and I haven't taken time to pull my life into harmony with what God is already doing out there, then how can I join God in what He is already about?" Through prayer God brings our lives into harmony with Who He is and what He is about, and then He asks us to follow.

I listened to a cassette tape recently that Nell Bruce, a powerful prayer partner, sent me. Nell Bruce had gone to visit Martha Franks, longtime missionary to China, to ask Miss Franks about her days in China and about a revival that happened there. Martha told this story on the tape: "It all began with missionary Marie Munson. While Marie was serving in China, she heard that there was a great revival in Korea and she wanted very much to go and see it. She felt that if she got to Korea, she could bring back to China a 'live coal' from the altar of revival in Korea to her province of Hunan. One day, as Marie was praying that the Lord would provide her money to go to Korea to see that revival, the Holy Spirit spoke to her and said, 'Marie, you don't need to go to Korea. What I have done there, I will do here in answer to prayer.' Marie said, 'Lord, if that is what You wish, and if that is what it will take to bring revival to China, I will do it.' She prayed for 20 years before revival came to her province."

Oh, that a "spiritual awakening" would come to America. Many people believe that we are not far from total "godlessness" in our country. What a difference you and I could make if we prayed on behalf of our nation and our world that God's Wind would blow fresh across our nation.

Are you willing to do that? Are you willing to bow your heart before God for 20 years on behalf of our nation?

Total Surrender

In His book, *If You Will Ask*, Oswald Chambers says, "The only one who prays in the Holy Spirit is the child, the child-spirit in us, the spirit of utter confidence in God. When we pray in the Holy Spirit we bring to God the things that come quite naturally to our minds, and the Holy Spirit who 'maketh intercession for the saints according to the will of God' (Romans 8:27) enables God to answer the prayer that He Himself prays in our bodily temples. 'That ye may be the children of your Father which is in heaven.' The Holy Spirit cannot delight in our wisdom; it is the wisdom of God He delights in."[1]

Have you ever seen a child, in utter dependance upon God, bow her head and ask God for something? I believe that is what God wishes for us to do—to have a child-like spirit as we pray through the Holy Spirit, who makes intercession for us. It's not because we're helpless that we pray. We pray because God is almighty. He is God.

Then we willingly surrender to be empowered by the Spirit. We bow our hearts before the Father and surrender our lives, our all, to Him. When we surrender, we "give over" or "give in," in this case to a power within us that is greater than anything we can do by ourselves. This is very difficult for us to do, for we live in a culture that tells us to look after number one, to look after ourselves, to do what's best for us, and to be in control. What Jesus asked us to do through the Holy Spirit is to give up control of our lives.

Jesus said to his disciples, "Come follow me." He did not say, "Decide for me." He asked them to yield or surrender to His authority in their lives. He asked them to give up everything. "Don't take anything with you. Don't take a second coat. Don't take a money bag. I'll walk before you and provide your needs," he said. That must have been simple for those disciples—fishermen, tax collectors, doctors, and other laymen He called, I sometimes think. After all, Jesus Himself called them. But even as I think that, the truth dawns on me that Jesus Himself has called me, too.

When I left Canada in 1955 to enroll in college, my father gave me a gift. My father said it was a jewel, and that the jewel would shine brighter and brighter and become more precious and priceless to me as the years past. The gift he gave me was Proverbs 3:5-6. It asks me to trust, lean on, and acknowledge Him, and then because He is a Covenant God, He tells me that if I will do that part, He will give me directions. Really, what He is asking me to do in that precious promise from the Proverbs is to surrender completely to Him. He wants me to bow my heart before Him and say to Him, "Father, what would You have me to do in this situation? God, lead me so that I will know what to do. I know what I want to do, but make me willing to put myself aside and surrender to Your will."

God also asks us to be obedient to Him. Obedience cannot come unless I am in such communion with the Holy Spirit that I am surrendered to hearing what He has to say and following Him.

I must confess that I understand this principle more from not having been obedient than from having been obedient to Him. When the Holy Spirit has nudged me to speak to someone about my personal relationship to Jesus or has put someone's name on my heart for prayer, I have dismissed it at times and thought, "I'll get to that later." At times like that I have been disobedient to the Spirit of God. When this happens I must bow before God, confess my sin, and let Him lead me back to obedience in Him.

Look at the life of Jesus. Before He did anything He would go away to pray. You know why—He knew where the Source of His power was. He said many times, "I do not do this in My own power; I do it in the power and authority of Him who sent Me." For us to be empowered, we must go to the Source of the power within us—the Holy Spirit. Whether we are driving in the car, ironing, doing dishes, making beds, or sitting quietly, we must pray, "Father, speak to me."

The Wind of God's Spirit

In Acts the Spirit of God came upon the church in such a powerful way that the people were "blown" out of it into Judea, Samaria, and the uttermost parts of the world. Jesus prayed for this to happen to us, too. "Sanctify them by the truth; your word is truth. As you sent me into the world, I have sent them into the world" (John 17:17-18 NIV).

The Spirit of God still wishes to blow through our lives today. We have an awesome responsibility to keep our lives such that the Spirit can blow through us to refresh someone else. This Spirit has blown through my life; has He blown through yours? My prayer for you is that you will understand who you are in Christ Jesus and that you will rely on Him, reclaim His calling on your life, risk to become involved in the world, bend your heart before Him, surrender your life, and be obedient to what He asks you to do. Remember, the

Holy Spirit is not a resource for the church in the world; the church (you and me) is the Holy Spirit's resource in the world.

I have never heard S. M. Lockridge preach, but I have heard several preachers quote him. One quote from him that I have heard is this: "If you decided to destroy the power of Jesus Christ, what would you use for power to destroy His power? If you destroyed the power of the Holy Spirit, you could not destroy the power of Jesus Christ or the Holy Spirit by fire, because He would refuse to burn. If you decided to destroy this power with water, He would walk on it. If you tried to destroy His power with a mighty wind, He would stand up on a boat and say, 'Peace be still, and it would lie down at His feet and lick His hand. What would you use to destroy His power? If you tried to use death, He'd clean out the grave and make it a decent place to wait for the resurrection. What would you use for power to destroy His power?" Listen fellow Christian, You are clothed in that power and that power is clothed in you. Claim it!

Jesus said in Matthew 28:18, "All power is given unto me in heaven and in earth" (KJV). All the power of God was invested in Jesus Christ and all the power of Jesus Christ is invested in the Church—you and me. We are the body of Christ in this world—the scattered body of Christ! When we bow our hearts before the Father in prayer, surrendering ourselves in obedience, we will be empowered by Him to be witnesses of what Jesus Christ has done in our lives.

Corrie Ten Boom said:

When man listens, God speaks.

When man obeys, God acts.

When man prays, God empowers.[2]

Empowered to rely. . . **Empowered** to reclaim. . . **Empowered** to risk in the name of the Holy Spirit. . . and if we claim that, a new wind, the wind of God's Spirit, will begin to blow. And when that happens. . .

My prayer is: God, clothe me in your Holy Spirit, and make me willing to bow my heart, to bend my knee, and to be obedient.

Notes

[1]Oswald Chambers, *If You Will Ask* (Grand Rapids: Discovery House, 1965), 57.
[2]Corrie Ten Boom, *Clippings from My Notebook* (Nashville: Thomas Nelson, Inc., 1982), 22.

Reflect Upon

1. Think about your prayer life. When you finish talking with the Father, do you feel empowered? What changes do you need to make in your prayer life?

2. Have you "centered" your life in Christ? Review what it means to center your life. Have you taken time lately to commune with God?

3. Has the Holy Spirit challenged you, through the reading of this book, to take a risk? What is He asking you to do?

Holy Spirit,

Clothe me with Yourself, dress Yourself with me, and make me Your resource in my world. Oh God, let my world see Your work through my life. I'm willing. Amen.

Teaching Plan
for Group Study

The purpose of this book is to lead readers to:
• determine a personal response to the Holy Spirit's leading
• reclaim the meaning of missions
• recognize entry points for personal involvement in missions and determine a plan of action for involvement
• acknowledge the diversity of the world and determine ways of involvement
• pray for a renewed reliance on the Holy Spirit's power.

The book is designed for either individual or group study. Individual study may be done by reading the book and completing the activities at the end of each chapter. The group study plans are given below. Church Study Course credit is available for either method of study.

Preparation

1. Read the book *Empowered!* Provide copies for study participants.
2. Consider the needs of the study participants. Select from the activities those which will meet the majority of their needs. Do not attempt to complete all the activities listed. They are only options.
3. Enlist small group leaders.
4. Gather materials needed to complete the activities. Prepare suggested handouts. Prepare a large banner with the word *Empowered!* printed on it and a large banner with the word *Missions* printed on it. Display these in study room.
5. Pray for a renewed sense of the Holy Spirit's empowering for yourself and all participants.

Large Group *(30 minutes)*

As participants enter, provide name tags. Distribute sheets of paper on which is printed the word *Empowered!* and these directions: Use this sheet to make notes during this study. After meeting fellow participants, move to the large "Missions" banner and write on it your definition of missions.

Convene the large group. Lead in a prayer for study participants and yourself. Close your prayer by reading Ephesians 3:20.

Read aloud some of the missions definitions from the banner. Summarize the preface of *Empowered!* Give a brief overview of the book as you mount strip posters of chapter titles to the *Empowered!* banner.

Choose from the following activities for the study of chapter 1:

• Ask participants to name symbols of the Holy Spirit. Review the ways Esther Burroughs refers to the Holy Spirit in chapter 1. Discuss these images.

• Clothe Me With Your Spirit—Enlist a participant to read Judges 6:34. Discuss what it means to be clothed in the Spirit.

• Ain't You Got Power?—Tell the stories of Dowella and Pitts and Ruth and Ida. Tell a personal story of how you have sensed the Holy Spirit's power in your life.

• Child-like Wonder—Ask participants to share times when they have felt wonder at the Holy Spirit's working.

• Signs and Wonders—Ask participants to read this section and call out characteristics or act of the Holy Spirit as they come across them. List these acts on a blackboard or poster board.

• God's Power Is God's Power—Enlist someone who has read *The Hiding Place* to tell about Corrie Ten Boom. Tell participants to write on the *Empowered!* handout the name of someone they know who responds in faith and obedience to the Spirit. Take time to pray silently in thanksgiving for these people.

• Do Not Quench the Spirit—Refer participants to the checklist on pages 18-19. Allow 5 minutes for a self-inventory.

Divide into smaller groups to discuss chapters 2 and 3.

Small Groups *(20 minutes)*

Display small posters or a flipchart of the outlines for chapters 2 and 3. Choose from the following activities for the study of chapter 2. Do the activities in small groups:

• Total Dependence—Ask participants to list emotions with which Esther dealt and discoveries she made as she dealt with her accident and recovery. Discuss her feelings.

• Total Surrender—Ask participants to read the section and discuss the word pictures of surrender that are included.

• Total Acceptance—Lead participants through Esther's walk of Ephesians 1:1-14. Ask someone to read aloud the poem on page 29.

• Total Power—Write a responsive reading based on Ephesians 3:20 and the content of this section.

Choose from the following activities for the study of chapter 3:

• Reclaiming the Call—Summarize the chapter introduction. Read or tell Debra Owens-Hughes' story. Discuss with participants how they feel when they are living out God's call.

• Reclaiming the Power—Summarize the section. Ask participants to discuss: (a) where they are in claiming the Spirit's power in their lives; (b) where their church(es) is (are) in claiming the Spirit's power. Discuss and list actions that participants can take to reclaim the Holy Spirit's power.

• Reclaiming Stewardship—Read aloud the story of the rich young ruler in Matthew 19:16-26, then consider the thoughts Esther lists on page 41. Ask participants to add their thoughts to the list.

• Discovering our Marketplaces—Summarize the section or enlist persons to read silently the stories of Sylvia and Ken and then tell the stories to the group. Lead participants to list the marketplaces they encounter. Spend time in prayer for the people present in these marketplaces.

• Reclaiming the Mission of the Church—Ask the group to respond to the questions included in the first paragraph. Summarize the remainder of the section. Conclude by assigning individuals the roles represented in "When, Lord" and ask them to read their lines aloud.

Individuals *(20 minutes)*

Tell participants to use this time to reflect silently on the questions at the end of chapters 1 through 3.

Partners *(20 minutes)*

Tell participants to select a partner for the study of chapter 4. Distribute handouts of the following questions. Leave space for answers. Instruct participants to read alternating sections, summarize them for their partners, and discuss the answers with their partners.

Recognizing and Providing Entry Points for Personal Involvement

• Crossing Barriers—What barriers in each story had to be overcome?
• The Little Things that Really Count—What "little things" can you do? Discuss possible first steps in ministry opportunities.
• Networking—What is networking? What networks do you have access to?
• Child of God/Priest of God—What entry points can you add to the list on pages 59-60?
• In Christ's Name—In what mission action projects is your church currently involved?

Tell participants to reconvene in small groups.

Small Groups *(20 minutes)*

Display on a small poster or a flipchart the outline for chapter 5. Summarize the chapter introduction.

Choose from the following activities for the study of chapter 5:
• Risking Through Prayer—Tell the story of Dorothy and Esther's prayer relationship. Display strip posters of facts on pages 65-66. Encourage participants to write two of the facts on their *Empowered!* handout and commit to pray daily and specifically for these needs.
• Multiplied Power—Summarize the section. Ask participants to voice their responses to the sentence: "It may require us to give up ownership in order to have partnership."
• Commitment—What Does It Mean?—On a small poster or flipchart, display the various definitions of commitment. After reviewing the section, ask participants to select or create the best definition.
• Risk Takers—Select three risk takers and tell their stories as though they were friends of yours.
• What is Jesus Christ's Address?—Ask participants the question, What is Jesus' address? Relate Dr. Parks' experience. Discuss his observation.

Individuals (*10 minutes*)

Tell participants to use this time to reflect silently on the questions at the end of chapters 4 and 5.

Large Group (*30 minutes*)

Choose from the following activities for the study of chapter 6:
• Centering on God—Define centering. Display on poster boards or a flipchart the quotes by T.W. Hunt and Henry Blackaby. Discuss the quotes. Summarize the story of Martha Franks.
• Total Surrender—Summarize the section.
• The Wind of God's Spirit—Enlist a reader with dramatic ability to read aloud the entire section.
Lead in a guided prayer experience. Tell participants that

you are going to read aloud the prayers at the close of each chapter with pauses between prayers. Explain that they are to spend time in silent prayer during the pauses. Conclude the prayertime by singing "Breathe on Me" (*Baptist Hymnal*, 1975 Edition).